NOT FAR FROM THE TRUTH

NOT FAR FROM THE TRUTH

AJABEYANG AMIN

Ajabeyang Publishing

Whoever has ears, let them hear. (Matthew 11:15 NIV)
For those with the hearts to listen and understand.

Contents

Introduction

Throughout my life, I have had many interactions that I've wanted to put in a bottle and keep. You know those light-bulb moment life changing conversations that move your heart to transformation? Those are the ones I'm talking about. Additionally, my work as a counseling psychologist is all about transformative dialogue. As a result, it made sense to write a book on conversations. Even though I will tell you that this idea did not come from me, it was all the Holy Spirit's work.

Going through my doctorate program, I completed a dissertation on mental health treatment approaches for African immigrants in the U.S. I conducted interviews with members of this group sharing their experiences of how they had gotten through grief, divorce, trauma, and the like. My dissertation committee was so impressed by my writing about the subject that they encouraged me to write a book. I already had the thought to do so, hence their words were affirmation. However, I didn't just want to write a research book because who would read it except us in the field?

I wanted a book that every and anyone could read regardless of their educational level. My other goal was that I wanted the reader to walk away with coping tools to help them with their mental, emotional, and spiritual wellbeing. How was I to do that? I wasn't sure.

Until somewhere right around the beginning of the Covid-19 pandemic, as I was thinking, praying, and reading my Bible, I noticed something. Jesus told many stories to help his listeners understand. So, there was one clue, "Ajab, tell stories." Then the other thought was, "Use your strengths." I am good at talking about emotions, thoughts, experiences, the things that make up people's inner worlds. Maybe it is because I am very in tune with my own.

So, all the thinking and praying led me to *Not Far from the Truth*, a book of short stories. Stories inspired by my research participants, friends, acquaintances, family members, and my own experiences. Although there are pieces of these people in every story, the 10 stories are fictional. They may feel so real because they are *not far from the truth*. You might find pieces of yourself in the stories as you read them. That is my hope.

How to read this book

Each of the 10 stories in this book is separate. Therefore, you can jump around if you like; pick whatever story is of interest and begin reading from there. If you are one of those people who likes to read from the beginning till the end, you can do that too. The book is organized to make it enjoyable reading from start to finish. There is a story for everybody, so feel free to share one or two of the stories with a friend or loved one who would relate.

My only appeal to you as you read is to sit with it! This is not a book to read in haste so you can move on to the next thing. It is a book to soak in and let it transform your heart and mind. I hope it does just that for you. Happy reading friends!

I

Fear of Disappointing African Parents

"But I thought you wanted to do medicine. You've been dreaming of this your whole life," Etienne told his son, Nkamji.

"No Papa, YOU'VE been dreaming of this my whole life. I didn't know what I wanted, and you got so excited when I liked the brain project in middle school. You walked around telling your friends that your son has the knack for science and will be a doctor someday. I didn't know what to say, so I decided to stick with it and see where it took me. But now after almost two years in college, I'm sure this is not what I want to do. Plus, my therapist says that I..."

"Your therapist? Since when do we see therapists? Is this therapist the one putting all this nonsense in your head?"

Nkamji started to notice that he was shutting down. His

words were escaping him, and he was forgetting his train of thought.

"Wait, wait, let him finish what he was saying," he heard his mother say. "Nkamji, continue, we are listening."

Nkamji replayed the role play in his mind. He and his therapist had gone through all the possibilities and had come up with a plan. This was the time, but his survival instinct to freeze was setting in. Remember to take a few deep breaths. Tell yourself slowly, "I am calm, I am calm, I am calm." See yourself as calm and collected. Think about what you want them to hear, you have no control over what they will say; focus on what you want them to know. Okay, let's try this again. He continued speaking:

"I have been thinking about my interests and my skills and..." He paused for a second... "And I think I want to be a psychologist. I have decided to change my major to psychology."

"A PSYCHOLOGIST? Isn't that a mad man''s doctor?" His father yelled while his mother tapped on his upper arm motioning him to relax. She had this way of calming her husband like only she could. This is why Nkamji had decided to tell her first, although his father didn't know that. Nkamji knew she would accept whatever he chose to study, but he was very worried about his father. His father's rage scared him.

When he described his concerns to his therapist, she proposed he have his mother as an ally when he had the conversation with his father. Nkamji thought this was a good idea, this gave him the push to tell his parents.

"Papa, if a psychologist is a mad man's doctor, then I guess I am a mad man. I've been seeing a psychologist for therapy. She works in the counseling and psychological services department at school. I found out from one of my friends that we get 10 free sessions as students each year, so I decided to try it. I didn't understand therapy at first and I didn't know what a psychologist does. But I understand a lot more about it now. There are various types of psychologists: clinical psychologists, counseling psychologists, engineering psychologists, educational psychologists, developmental psychologists, forensic psychologists, health psychologists, neuropsychologists. I can still do research on the brain, and I can also provide therapy to those in need. I'm not sure what type of psychologist I want to be yet, but I know that clinical psychologists are the ones who work with people who have severe mental illnesses like the people we used to see roaming the streets half naked back home. These people's mental illnesses were not being managed and so they became worse and out of control. I want to be a solution to these types of issues, Papa. I would still be a doctor because I would need a doctorate to be a psychologist, but just not a medical doctor. You can say I'll be something like a mental doctor."

His father looked at his mom with a loss of words, then looked back at Nkamji. Something about what Nkamji was telling him sounded compelling. He could tell the boy had done his research and he sounded confident and even persuasive. Etienne knew his son was the quiet type, for him to say all these things to him was a big deal. He didn't know how to respond. And his pride reminded him not to give in so quickly. What about all the years of him dreaming of his son as a medical doctor? Does he just forget about that? The thoughts were happening so quickly even he didn't know all of what was happening. But he was listening to his son. He took a look at him and for a split second he noticed that Nkamji wasn't in primary school anymore. He saw a young man in front of him telling him something he cared about. How had he not noticed any of this prior? How does he respond to this now? His wife seemed supportive, but Etienne had had multiple dreams of his son in a white coat. What does all this mean?

It was as if the four seconds were taking an eternity. Nkamji wasn't sure if he should keep talking or if he should wait for someone to say something. Although he felt the tension in his chest, he also felt relieved. The cat was out of the bag, now he was waiting for a response. If only they knew what he had been through to get here, just to have this conversation...

The back story

Nkamji was the last child with two older sisters. He spent the first 8 years of his life in Buea, Cameroon, then his parents migrated to Pennsylvania, U.S. He was told he has a sharp memory because he remembers a lot about Buea, like how he used to go next door to play with his neighbors and how they liked climbing the mango and guava trees in his compound. Growing up in America felt strange especially during his teenage years. There seemed to be life at home and life outside of home, which were two very different worlds. At home, he was "Nkamji" who had to respect his elders, not talk back, do his chores, do his homework, basically do the right thing, which is whatever his parents told him to do. At school, he was "Kamji" or "Nakamji" or "Nankamji" or "Nekamji." His teachers and friends couldn't get the humming N sound to begin his name, so he got accustomed to them mispronouncing his name. He even started introducing himself with the wrong pronunciation because he was tired of having to explain how to say it. "Let's just make it easy on them," he thought. In school, his teachers told him to speak up, express his opinion, be bold, to even think out loud.

The things he could do at school that were praised were the same things that he could never try at home. Nkamji often found himself internally conflicted, yet he didn't like to upset his father who had high expectations of him as his only son. His father would remind him and his siblings, "my house, my rules," which seemed counter to Nkamji's eight grade teacher asking him, "What do you want to learn this year?" Nkamji thought, "shouldn't you be telling us that?" He wouldn't dare say anything of course, but it just seemed odd to him that his teacher was asking for the student's opinions on what she should teach. The really odd question was during mental health month when she asked, "How do you respond emotionally when you're in a difficult situation?" He didn't quite understand the question then. But he heard his classmates say things like, "I feel scared, and it makes me want to run away." "Sometimes I feel a sudden stomachache and it is almost as if my chest starts to get tight." Nkamji had never thought about emotional reactions or even body sensations until he heard other people describing things he experienced. Among other things, the teacher talked about deep breathing exercises that could help. This was the first time he got an inkling that he could do something about the stressful reactions he thought were part of his norm.

It was almost two years that Nkamji had been in college at Penn State University. He set out to study Pre-Med as his parents had wanted, but during his first semester, he began to doubt if he had chosen the right major. His dissatisfaction grew each semester, and he would tell himself, "I could be doing something else." But then he would imagine the lecture when he told his parents he wanted to switch majors and he would decide every time that it wasn't worth the heartache. He was going to push through, complete the degree, graduate, and then do what he wants. The problem was Nkamji knew he wanted to work with people, but he had no idea what he wanted to do. How would he tell his parents that he wanted to switch majors without having the answer for what he would do instead? He felt stuck.

As time lapsed, his grades started to slip. Nkamji, who was known to be an A student was barely passing his courses. He couldn't bring himself to sit down and study when he knew this was not what he wanted to do. His academic advisor proposed that he change his major to undeclared and take primarily general education courses while he decided on a major. That was close to the end of his first year. He was worried about what his parents would say so he decided to stick with Pre-med.

Nkamji started to isolate himself from his friends, feeling the shame of not being a good student. It seemed his friends were excelling and moving forward while he was conflicted and stuck. As much as he tried to tell himself, "You are smart, you can do this, just a few more years to go," his body told him something else, "You don't like this, you could be doing something much more enjoyable." Whenever he spoke with his parents and they asked him, "How is school? How are your classes?" he would have the thought, "should I tell them the truth or should I not?" Over and over, he would wrestle and give in to the latter, "Don't you dare tell them, remember all of what they have done for you to get you to college, all the tuition they have spent already. And what will you tell them you are going to do instead? That you are going to help people? How? You don't even know the answer to that." So, he would keep quiet and say, "School is fine." And his parents would say, "That's good," as if they didn't really want him to have any other answer. Nkamji didn't realize his frustration was growing. He started staying up late into the morning playing video games and then sleeping through his classes the next morning, which only increased the failed grades. Feeling more shame, guilt, and disappointment in himself, he concluded, "I can't recover from this, there is no way I'm telling my parents now."

On his way to class one Monday afternoon, Nkamji heard someone call him. He turned around and saw Kinti from the African Student Association (ASA).

"Nkamji, long time. Where have you been? We've been asking about you."

"I'm here, I'm fine. How are you doing?"

"I'm okay. I was just on my way to CAPS for my appointment."

"CAPS? What's that?"

"Counseling and psychological services. I'm going for a therapy session."

"Oh oh my advisor has mentioned that to me. So how is it?"

"It's really helped me. I've been going since my freshman year. I might as well make use of my free sessions, right?"

"Wait! They are free?"

"Yes oh! We are already paying for them in our tuition, so we get a number of sessions free every year. I think it's about 10 or so. I hear some schools don't even have a limit to the number of sessions they get each year. Are you thinking of going?"

"Nah! How is sitting and talking to someone going to help me? I can talk to my friends."

"Do you talk to your friends though? I haven't seen you in like a month and we are in the same class."

Nkamji laughed and said, "Touché touché!"

"I used to think the same thing before and you know us Africans, we're not used to it. But as my therapist says, what's the worst thing that can happen? Plus, I needed the support, and it is free. Where else are you going to get free therapy or therapy my parents are already paying for?"

"I didn't know it was free. But I don't know about this Kinti."

"Think about it this way, has what you've been doing been working for you?"

"Ah beg leave me[2]. Are you the well-being police now?"

"Hahaha... noo please, I'll leave you oh. It's just that since I started going, I've been advocating for more people to go especially my African brothers and sisters on campus. Many people don't know about the service, and it could help us even with adjusting to life on campus and in this country, you know. But let me leave you Nkamji. Do you! I'll see you some other time? Maybe in class on Wednesday?"

"Yeah, see you Kinti."

Nkamji thought about it afterward. Kinti was right, he wasn't talking to anyone, and it was obvious that he needed help. He was failing, he wasn't going to classes, he wasn't going to ASA meetings or gatherings, he wasn't even talking to his roommate anymore. Maybe, he will try it next month.

Two weeks passed, Nkamji wasn't doing any better when he came to see his academic advisor. "Nkamji, would you like me to walk with you to CAPS? I'll be happy to show you where it is," his advisor told him.

"Ehm I don't think that would be necessary," Nkamji told him.

"Will you go immediately after our time here then?"

"Sure sure, I will go." This time Nkamji had actually decided to go for therapy.

It was initially difficult for him to express himself during the therapy session. After the first few sessions, his therapist assessed that he was feeling hopeless and helpless about what to do regarding his major, which contributed to depression and anxiety. He felt anxious when he thought about talking to his parents, fearful that he would disappoint them, hence he didn't tell them what was going on. He felt so miserable studying Pre-med that he couldn't even bring himself to do it anymore. And he was upset with himself for letting this drag on for so long till the point of him failing. He was angry at himself for not acting sooner even though he knew Pre-med wasn't what he wanted. All these factors kept Nkamji constantly worrying, feeling bad about himself and his life, thus isolating and distancing himself from friends. Things that he used to enjoy doing felt tasteless and meaningless.

A few sessions in, Nkamji was still waiting for his therapist to tell him what to do. He wanted a formula to get out of his depression. Instead, she would ask him questions like "What is the worst thing that could happen if you told your parents the truth? Will they disown you?"

"No, they wouldn't do that," he would respond.

"Would they stop paying for your education?"

"No, they wouldn't do that."

"Ok, so there are no tangible repercussions to you changing your major?"

"They will be angry, very angry, especially my dad. He will be disappointed in me."

"Nkamji, it is not your job to manage your dad's feelings," she will tell him. "I understand this is difficult for students from collectivistic cultures that place a high value on respecting their elders and working for the good of the family. Many students such as yourself find themselves stuck. You have to decide for yourself if you want to live to please them, which is an option or if you want to start voicing your opinion. It's up to you. It seems you have tried the first option for a long time, and you are miserable doing it. How about trying a different option and seeing what happens?"

Nkamji and his therapist would explore all the possibilities of what could happen and what he could do about it. But Nkamji was still so frightened by their reaction and wouldn't tell them. Meanwhile Nkamji was getting frustrated with his therapist. Why did he still feel anxious and depressed?

A few months into therapy, his therapist asked him while they were talking,

"Nkamji, what do you want?"

He sat for a second quietly with his mind racing. Something about her question made him realize that she couldn't change him; he had to start taking some actions in order to get better. If the worst thing his parents could do was get angry and even be disappointed in him, why was he so afraid? They wouldn't disown him, they wouldn't stop supporting him, they would just be very angry. After this enlightenment, Nkamji and his therapist began working on how to approach his parents. He decided that he would tell them when he went home during Spring break. Plus, he had a better idea of what he wanted to do with his life.

Present conversation with parents

So here he was standing in front of his father and mother telling them that he was changing his major.

Etienne knew he would have to relent someday. He didn't know the day would come so quickly. He looked at Nkamji, "I have to think about this" was all he could muster up to say.

Chapter Notes

[1]In Cameroon and other parts of Africa, people who have severe mental illnesses are referred to as "mad man" or "man woman." "Mad" is equivalent to "crazy."

[2]Speaking in Pidgin English meaning "Please, leave me."

2

Lessons From Nana's Godmother

I often tell myself that when I grow up, I want to be just like Aunty Agnes. I don't see what Uncle Boniface means when he says she is a quiet woman. I always see her dancing or humming to some tune. Sometimes I hear her laugh out so loud that I think her stomach would explode. Uncle Boni[3] makes her laugh like this. I like them together. They are the only couple I know whom I admire. If I get married someday, I want to be like Aunty Agi[4] and Uncle Boni. Don't get me wrong, they're not perfect. They have disagreements to the point where their faces would be so solemn when I come to visit. But I've seen them make up. Uncle Boni would come to her and say, "I'm sorry chérie coco[5]. You're right, I shouldn't have said it in that way. I was angry." And Aunty Agi would stop whatever she was doing and face him. I would see them exchange a few more words of apologies and affection and then give each other a kiss. And it was over. They were back to their normal selves. Sometimes I wondered why they didn't wait till I was gone before they made up. Weren't they embarrassed to be doing all that in front of me? Apparently, they didn't care. It seemed like whatever argument they had was eating both of them up so much that they needed to clear the air before it destroyed them. Aunty Agi herself told me that she hated keeping grudges or hard feelings towards anyone especially her husband. She didn't care whatever it took for them to settle the conflict and move on. She also told me that some of their problems didn't get resolved, but they understood each other and that was enough for her. She knew that Uncle Boni had a whole life before they met so she couldn't change him and she wasn't trying to, she just wanted him to care about her opinion and the things she cared about.

Among all my Cameroonian aunties and uncles, she was the only one who actually took the time to speak to me like an adult. It didn't matter how old I was. She would tell me, "I wish someone had told me these things before I went to high school. I wouldn't have made all the stupid mistakes I made." She was talking about everything, relationships, finances, sex; yes we even spoke about sex. The first time I asked her a question related to sex and body parts was when I was in Class 2 in primary school[6]. Aunty Agi didn't even flinch, she just gave me the answer and I said, "okay" and kept going. Since then, we have had several conversations about boys and sex. She does not tell me everything of course. She would ask me questions and then she would answer some of mine. She would say, "Eh! my curious one. If you don't have the answers you will continue to itch." She's right. I have always been curious, and I know who to go to when I have questions about anything. Aunty Agi is my go-to-person.

I'm not sure why she indulges my curiosity, but I suspect that it is because of her own past. Aunty Agi had a child when she was 16. She never got married until she was 48 years old. Her son, Yannick works in the film industry in Atlanta. I don't know what he does honestly, but I can tell he really likes it. I've met him a few times, he seems nice, and he loves his mom very much, but I don't know him that well. What I know is that Aunty Agi had him in Cameroon right after she finished the GCE Ordinary Level[7] in Our Lady of Lourdes Secondary School[8]. The whole Lourdes girls and Sacred Heart boys' connection is what brought Yannick's dad and Aunty Agi together. His dad went to Sacred Heart College[9] where they had met 2 years prior. Aunty Agi said they liked each other, but they didn't know what they were doing at the time. When she got pregnant, he was out of the picture. Aunty Agi told me all the shame she endured from her parents, relatives, and peers. Her parents supported her and helped her raise him while she finished her Advanced Level[10] a little later than she had hoped. She said Yannick was the turning point of her life and played a major role in giving her direction. Aunty Agi came to Georgia 12 years ago, a few years before my family moved. She told me it was hard for her in the beginning. She missed everything about home, but she adjusted. She was like part of our family. I always saw these young girls stopping by her house or calling her for something. I would ask her, "How do you know so many young people?" And she would respond, "This is what I prayed for, to help youngsters like yourself. God leads them to me. I can't even tell you how I met half of them. Whenever you decide to serve God, He will provide the opportunities for you."

Aunty Agi's life seemed very full. I never heard her complain about not being married. Actually, I didn't think she would get married, but she met Uncle Boni 5 years ago. They've been married for 4 years now.

You know what is funny? Aunty Agi is not even related to me. She is Mami[11]'s best friend. She always took it upon herself to be my godmother. Nobody gave her that title, but that's how I think of her. Mami doesn't like the term "godmother" because she thinks people don't use it well. Mami says godmothers are supposed to instill God in their godchildren, teach them how to apply the scriptures in real life, and act as spiritual guides to their godchildren. Instead, people just like to be able to say, "I am so so and so's godmother." "What a waste of a great opportunity!" She would say.

When Mami and Aunty Agi were younger, they told themselves that if they had children, they would play the role of spiritual guides in each other's children's lives. Sure, Mami knew that Aunty Agi was not planning to have any other children, but she tried to be there for Yannick as much as she could. And Aunty Agi has been there for Clarisse and I since we were born. Clarisse hasn't taken to her as much as I have. Maybe because she isn't as curious as I am, I don't know. Me, I love me some Aunty Agi. Her house is my second home here in Georgia and I make it my goal to visit or talk to her at least once every week.

One of my favorite things about Aunty Agi is that she tells it like it is, but she doesn't really tell me what to do. She doesn't have a problem telling me no when she doesn't want to give me something, but I know she loves me anyway.

Let me tell you about my last visit to Aunty Agi's...

Uncle Boni let me into the house and told me that Aunty Agi was in the kitchen. I could smell something stewing as I walked closer to the kitchen. I could hear Aunty Agi singing along to a song and I walked into her moving her hips to the beat.

"Hello Aunty," I said.

"Heeey Nana," she said still moving to the beat of the song. She moved closer to me and gave me a hug as she swayed to the music and asked, "Do you know this one? I mean the song."

"Ehm of course, who doesn't know *Coucou* by *Charlotte Dipanda*?" I said with a smirk on my face.

"You see the girl? All you youngsters listening to *Ginger me, Joro, Essence*, and the like. I thought you wouldn't know the classy Charlotte. I just love her sound."

"Yeah, me too! I love her voice."

"I know, it's lovely, isn't it? How are you, dear?"

"Aunty, I have a dilemma." I've gotten into the habit of not beating around the bush with Aunty Agi because she gets it out of me sooner or later. She isn't in the business of wanting to hear, "Fine, and you?" She always wants me to give it to her for real. Whenever I give her a "fine and you?" She would say, "I can tell you all about how I am doing, but how are you really? I don't need the niceties." We had been through this several times until I came to the conclusion that I would just be honest about how I was doing on the first try.

"Oh oh! Tell me all about it," she said.

"Well, you remember Uncle Divine?"

"The one who calls you when he needs something?"

"Yes! He called me again and I can't bring myself to pick up the phone. I know he is going to ask me how I am doing, how school is going, and then he is going to ask me to send a little something for him. I don't know what to say to him. I don't want to send him anything. I also want him to stop asking me for money when I am barely making anything myself. Sometimes I feel like that is the only reason he calls me, just to fund him. He doesn't even know much about my life. It seems people back home just think that once you come to America, you make a lot of money, and you have lots to spare. They don't know we have bills and responsibilities and sometimes we have to work multiple stupid jobs just to make ends meet. Aunty, me I'm tired."

"Weh ashia[12]! I'll be tired too if I were you."

"You know one of my Nigerian friends was telling me that it is the same thing with her cousins back home. They always call her to ask her for money. When my friend asked them what they can do to make some money so that they aren't depending on her, the response one of them said was something like, "I don't know, things are tough here..." As if America is not tough too. What do they think? That we are just here hanging out with Jeff Bezos?"

"Hahaha... you are funny!"

"No Aunty, it's not funny, it's annoying. Even more so because I want to help. If I had money, I would give Uncle Divine. I also want to send money to my cousins and friends, but I can't afford to give them because I still have to pay rent and bills. And I'm still in college. So, I feel guilty when I say no. So, I just prefer to avoid them."

"How is that working out for you?"

"It's not! I keep thinking about having to call them back. It bothers me."

"Do they know that life is tough for you? Have you told them?"

"Eh eh Aunty! Why would I tell them?"

"Because life is tough for you, and you want them to stop asking you for money when you are a struggling student. You see, that's the problem. Many of us here want to put on a facade to our friends back home that we are doing well. We are contributing to the same problem we complain about. We make it seem like we have money because we are in America, but then when people ask us for money, we are angry at them for assuming that we don't have to work very hard for it and pay lots of bills."

"True true Aunty, you have a point. But what should I do?"

"That's the other problem, you acting as if you have no control over the situation and these things are happening to you. Take responsibility, be honest with them and tell them the truth. Life is hard for you too; you have rent and bills to pay and you don't have enough money this month or this year. Have conversations with them so they can get to see how life is here. It's not all roses, help them understand that. I mean you don't have to explain your life story if you don't want to but think about how much you want them to know about you and tell them. Like any of us, sometimes you have money, sometimes you don't. Give when you do and say no when you don't."

"Aunty, you make it sound so easy."

"Because it is! We make it more complicated for ourselves. What would happen if you told Uncle Divine, 'Uncle, I don't make that much because I'm still in school and I have bills to pay. I don't have enough money to give to you?' Wouldn't that relieve you instead of all the time you are spending worrying about it? And wouldn't that help him to move on instead of waiting to see what you would say? Why prolong the time both of you are bothered when you could end it quickly?"

"Well, when you put it like that, it makes sense."

"Is he depending on you to take care of his responsibilities? Is Uncle Divine the type of person who is working really hard, but he doesn't have enough or is he sitting outside in front of the bar chatting and drinking beer when his family is hungry? Is your uncle a sluggard?"

At this Aunty Agi started laughing hysterically, it surprised me. "I'm glad you are finding some humor in this."

Catching her breath, she exclaimed, "Sorry Nana, I just find it very funny whenever the book of Proverbs talks about sluggards. God is so funny eh! I read some things in His Word, and it makes me laugh. How did He choose to describe things like that? Like the one that says a sluggard puts his hand in a jar and he won't bring it out to his mouth or something like that... oh Nana, it's so funny."

She snickered for a short while before she continued.

"Okay okay, what was I even saying? Your uncle! Yes, your uncle what type of person is he? You might not even know the answer to that question. Whatever type of person he is, his problems are bigger than you. You can't fix them. And it is not your responsibility to provide for him. If he is the hard-working type and you have money, help him if you can. If he is the lazy type, giving him money will enable his laziness. If you don't know how your uncle is, ask your mom."

I thought she was finished, but then she added, "Talk to him and get to know where he is coming from and help him to know where you are coming from too. I know we Africans sometimes, it's hard to do that especially with an uncle. If you don't want to go that deep with Uncle Divine, decide for yourself what you will do and do it without questioning him."

"Hmm! That sounds fair. When he calls me, I'm usually too annoyed to have a conversation, I'm just answering questions, "yes," "fine," and waiting to hear what he is going to ask me. I guess I can actually ask him more questions about his life, and I can tell him more about my life."

"Eh he!" Aunty Agi responded, then she asked me, "Tell me something, why do you feel guilty when you say no to people back home?"

"Hmm..." I had to think about that question for a few seconds before I replied, "Because I know that I am better off than them. And isn't that part of being able to give back when you have been given so much? I know that God has blessed me, I am in America, I will be done with my university education in 2 years. Some people don't have as much as I do. Doesn't the Bible say we should give cheerfully?"

"Oh, I see what's happening. You are comparing your life with theirs and you think you are better than them because you are here, and they are there. So, you need to help them or else you are doing something wrong. You think God has blessed you with a lot and He hasn't blessed them? My dear, such thinking will not help in your giving cheerfully. This is the type of thinking that causes many westerners to go to the developing world to "save them" because they think they are so poor when they have not understood what the people actually have or what they value, not to talk of what they need."

I must have struck a nerve with Aunty Agi because she had a lot to say about this. She continued speaking.

"Don't get me wrong, I am not saying that you don't have privileges as compared to people in many parts of the world including other people here in America. That's not the point. Your assumption that you are better off because of your privileges of being in America carries this mentality of "I am better than you," which is not a good place to give from. It leaves you feeling superior and gives you the impression that they need you. You probably also make them feel that they need you to be better off instead of them finding solutions to solve their own problems."

"I guess I never thought of it that way," I told her. She was right, I did think I was better off than many of them because I am in America. I had to sit with that for a little while before I said.

"Okay okay Aunty, I get your point. You want me to realize that nobody is better than the other and you want me to take responsibility."

"You're getting it. Doesn't Acts 17 say God determines the times and places where we should live? It is no mistake they are in Cameroon, and you are here. And you are not better because of it. We each have a purpose wherever we are, and we can make the most out of any situation."

She continued, "A better way is for each of us to accept where we are, take responsibility for what we can, ask for help when we need it, and give out of what we have not out of obligation or guilt. Plus, you can't give out of what you don't have. This is what leads to people milking themselves dry because they're trying so hard to give when they don't have the resources themselves. You don't have money for your monthly expenses and then you take the small money you have and give to someone else. Where does that leave you? Will you have more money next time when you are homeless?"

"I guess not!"

"To go back to you referring to the Bible saying to be a cheerful giver, let's look at it. Do you want to pull it up on your phone or go grab my Bible?"

"I have it right here Aunty."

Here is another thing I have learned during my time with Aunty Agi. She always has me pulling out my Bible. After my first few times of blundering saying I don't have a Bible or Bible app, I learned that this wouldn't stop her. She would have me go get hers, download some Bible app or Google search something. So, I have learned to be ready.

"Ok great." She said, "Read 2 Corinthians 9:7-12. Read it out loud." So, I did.

"Each of you should give what you have decided in your heart to give, not reluctantly or under compulsion, for God loves a cheerful giver. And God is able to bless you abundantly, so that in all things at all times, having all that you need, you will abound in every good work. As it is written: "They have freely scattered their gifts to the poor; their righteousness endures forever." Now he who supplies seed to the sower and bread for food will also supply and increase your store of seed and will enlarge the harvest of your righteousness. You will be enriched in every way so that you can be generous on every occasion, and through us your generosity will result in thanksgiving to God. This service that you perform is not only supplying the needs of the Lord's people but is also overflowing in many expressions of thanks to God."

"Nana, what do you see?"

"Each person should give what they have decided to give... ehm Aunty there is a lot in here, please explain it!"

"Hahaha! Why are you giving up when you haven't even tried?" She asked me.

Then she said.

"It's okay, there is a lot here so let me explain. First, it is important to know that this passage is just a section of a letter that was written to a family of believers in Corinth. It was written to encourage this church in multiple ways.

In this section, Paul is encouraging them to be generous. When you read passages like this or anything in the Bible for that matter, understand that there is a context of the time and the situation. And there is the actual principle that it is stating. Then, we have to ask ourselves, how can we apply this to my particular situation today? Sometimes you need to read the whole book of Corinthians to better understand the message, so you don't take things out of context like many people do. Are you following?"

"Yes Aunty, please continue."

"It starts off by saying what you started saying, give what you have decided in your heart. In other words, check your heart to make sure you are not giving from a place of reluctance or compulsion or guilt as we have already talked about. Instead, give cheerfully! God loves when we give happily. The passage goes on to describe how God can supply your needs so that you can continue to do good. One of the natural consequences of giving is feeling good, but it is not the reason why we give. What do you see in the passage that describes why we give?"

"Hmm... let me see... I give so that hmm... people will give thanks to God."

"Yes, my dear, that's it. God uses us to supply each other's needs, and ultimately it all points back to people glorifying God through thanksgiving."

"Wow! I see."

"Your giving should bring people closer to thanksgiving. Of course, there is more in this passage we can talk about, but for now let's just focus on this."

"I didn't really think about it that way. I'm mostly thinking about what people will think of me if I don't help them."

Aunty Agi looked at me with her compassionate eyes, "Well, you live and you learn right?"

For a short while we both didn't say anything as I reread the passage silently. I could hear the soft music still playing in the background. Then Aunty Agi asked, "So do you know what you will do about your Uncle Divine's phone calls?"

"Well, this is making me realize that rather than avoiding them, I need to call him back and tell him I don't have money at this time. Aunty, I actually think I need to do better at budgeting my money so I can have a benevolence fund like you had told me some time ago that you and Uncle Boni have. That way I am prepared to give cheerfully, and I know when to say no if the fund is empty. Isn't that a good idea?

"That's a great idea, hun. It allows you to manage your responsibilities and give cheerfully as well. So, do you want some fufu corn, njama njama, and kati kati[13]?"

"Yes, of course. Thank you, Aunty! What would I do without you?"

"You'll be just fine, my dear."

Chapter Notes

[3] Boni is short for Boniface

[4] Agi is short for Agnes

[5] Is an endearing phrase in French Africa that translates to "sweetheart" or "darling"

[6] This is equivalent to 1st grade in elementary school

[7] First level of examinations originating from British system and common in English speaking parts of Africa. This exam is the 1st of 2 to determine preparedness for university.

[8] All girls Catholic boarding school in Bamenda, Cameroon

[9] All boys Catholic boarding school in Bamenda, Cameroon

[10] The second exam to determine preparedness for university

[11] An expression for mother

[12] An expression of empathy common throughout Cameroon

[13] A popular Cameroonian dish of corn millet, vegetables, and chicken stew

3

Reclaiming Life After Divorce

It had been almost 6 months since Thabiti's divorce from his wife of 18 years. He was trying to forget Zawadi, but thoughts kept swirling in his mind, "I miss her, I hate her." Followed by, "Remember how much you two fought. Plus, she hates you. She moved on. She's already dating another man, remember." How was he just supposed to pick up and move on from the life they had? How did she do it? He could feel his anger rising, "After all I did for her. After all the sacrifices."

Moving from Tanzania to America was no easy feat and they had gone through the journey together. A few years in, Zawadi became interested in nursing and both of them decided that Thabiti would work while she went to nursing school. He was excited for her and was willing to help pay for some of her education. He thought, "Why not? In the long run, her doing work that she likes would make their family stronger." He never expected her to move on so quickly. They were separated for a few years, but the divorce was only finalized last year, and she was already in another man's arms. Apparently, they had been dating for much longer. How dare she! How could she?

Feelings of shame washed over him as he thought about his honor and respect. "What will people think? I wasn't man enough to keep my wife, to the point where she had to find someone better than me." People were already saying that he was soft for letting his wife have so much freedom in their relationship, but that never bothered Thabiti. He wasn't the kind to rule over anyone, he preferred a partnership. Now, what did he have left? He felt he had lost everything, well almost everything. Thank God they had shared custody of their two kids. But she took the house. "My house!" Thabiti was seething.

His thoughts were going wild, and he felt an upsurge of pressure as he thought, "It would have been better if she were dead." At least he wouldn't have to see her again, he wouldn't have to know what she was doing, he wouldn't have to bear the shame of the fact that she left him.

His suffering was too great, and he wanted her to feel some of what he was feeling. She could not be happy when he was so miserable. "Actually, I wish I were dead," he thought. "No more pain, I'll be out of this misery." But what about the children? He loved his children. And if he was honest with himself, he still cared for Zawadi. His mind flashed back to all the stories she showed him of what he used to think didn't occur within the African community.

They involved a series of suicides and homicides of African men killing their wives, and in some cases their children and themselves. In 2018 in Chicago,[14] a Nigerian man killed his Cameroonian wife and 7-year-old daughter, and then himself leaving two children as orphans. The same year, a Kenyan couple[15] was found dead in their New Jersey apartment leaving three children behind. In 2020, there was a Cameroonian murder-suicide[16] case in Cincinnati that left three surviving children. There was another incident of a Ghanaian pastor who shot his wife[17] in Florida. Zawadi was so intrigued by these cases. Her curiosity led her to find out that a Nigerian nurse created a hotline[18] to prevent further murders after hearing of 10 cases of Nigerian women in the U.S. being killed by their partners between a two-year span. Zawadi used to tell him the news expressing her disgust for men who were too proud to let their wives have their own careers and make more money than them. She felt these men became so enraged as their wives gained more of their voice that they felt emasculated and resorted to killing their families.

Zawadi had an air of confidence. It was one of the reasons he was attracted to her. She knew who she was and could stand her ground when she needed to. But she took things too far. She became pompous. Their conflicts increased. It became his way, or her way and she wouldn't relent. He wasn't willing to concede either. Back home in Tanzania, this is when a family member or friend would come in to help them, but the closest family member was five hours away from Massachusetts by flight. They had friends, but they didn't really get involved. And even when some family and friends tried to intervene, it just wasn't the same as if they were back home. They couldn't resolve their problems and things kept getting worse. They could see their issues were affecting the kids who were now 9 and 11 years old. Zawadi had first mentioned she wanted to separate, and Thabiti thought they would get some space for some time, then work things out. But it didn't get better, so she filed for divorce. It was as if the rug was being pulled from under him and he didn't have a chance to catch himself before the fall. Thabiti never thought he would get a divorce, but here he was. He was sad and scared to admit that he could relate to those men whom Zawadi used to make fun of. He too had thoughts of ending it all. But he knew he couldn't do it. He loved Zawadi too much and would never think of hurting his children any more than their divorce already did.

Thabiti thought about calling Baraka. At least he would have a good time partying and drinking, that's all Baraka had been doing since his divorce. But he knew better. He knew that Baraka was numbing his own pain with alcohol and parties. Thabiti was no fool. Baraka called him once to express his anger about what his ex-wife said to him. When Thabiti tried to talk more about it, Baraka was quick to change the subject saying he didn't want to waste time on this. But Thabiti could tell he was angry and hurt. He never heard Baraka talk about any other feelings about his divorce. It seems Baraka had this idea that men were supposed to be tough and stoic. Talking about feelings was a waste of time and energy. He would say, "I'm free, I'm happy, it's over, it had to be over. That woman was a witch." Thabiti knew Baraka couldn't help him. This meant it was time!

It was time for Thabiti to ask Gatimu about this group he was a part of. They were a group of about eight divorced men who talked about their struggles. Thabiti wasn't very interested in sharing his stories with other people, but the fact that he had thoughts of death scared him a little. He decided he might as well go and sit in and hear what other people had to say.

Divorced men's group one week later

The room was quite spacious. There were 10 chairs arranged in a circular fashion. Thabiti didn't know what to expect except what Gatimu had told him. Gatimu and his college friend started the group two months ago. After their divorces, they spent a lot of time talking about it and thought to open their conversations to their male friends and friends of friends going through divorce. There was no pressure to share. They just wanted to offer men a place to talk about their divorce. Thabiti liked that there were no rules about sharing for he thought, "What should I say? Hello, my name is Thabiti, I've had thoughts about my ex-wife and I being dead." What would they think of him? That he was crazy?

The group was supposed to start at 7pm, but many walked in 10 to 15 minutes late. "African time! I'm in good company," he thought. He didn't know anyone in the group except Gatimu, but everyone seemed friendly.

After pleasantries and brief introductions, a tall dark man was the first to start talking:

"I shared this with my counselor once: I was listening to somebody explain how veterans return from active combat. They've lived there, they've had this community of soldiers who have their back, and they are in it together. Then they come back home and that goes away and they start missing it. They go crazy and they long for it, which makes their families even more resentful thinking, 'You left us, you were in danger, we were worried about you all the time, and then you come back home and you want to go back? What's wrong with you?' But he said the only people who understand what it's like to return from combat and miss it are people who are divorced."

The room was quiet as almost everyone nodded in agreement.

Then, a short plump man said:

"There are so many days when I'm like, "Oh I miss her or I miss this." But then I'm like, but it was toxic, it was killing me, the relationship wasn't healthy for me. But I miss it, I miss her, she hates you, you can't go back to her... It is a feeling of waking up and not having an arm or a leg after many years. For 15 years, I've been waking up next to somebody I've known so well, we have all these inside jokes, we can finish each other's sentences, all these things. It's like half of my brain is gone. I wake up like, Oh there is nobody next to me and it's quiet in the house. It starts feeling like the walls are closing in."

The first man who spoke added some more details about his story:

"We met 25 years ago and pretty much went from college to being married and there were a lot of things we had in common. We really worked well together, but underneath the surface there were a bunch of things happening. Over time I understood all this from talking to my counselor. The things we had set in place in our 20s, the power dynamics and all that stuff, when I began trying to change them in my 30s, it just wasn't working because she was used to having her way and I was used to letting her have her way. As I began getting more assertive, we began clashing all the time and she eventually said no, she couldn't live like that and she left."

A young handsome man whom Thabiti wondered why he was there said:

"Initially after the divorce, I wasn't looking forward to going home at the end of the day. I would go talk to friends, play pool, I would stay out during the summer. I began getting into more activities, playing volleyball, or stuff like that just because I didn't want to go home because it was too empty and too quiet. I wasn't used to that. But I've also been going for counseling for a while so that's been helping me to reconcile with the fact that I have a new reality to live, so I'm slowly getting used to it. I don't know if it's harder or if it's easier really. We have two kids, and we co-parent. I see them two to three times a week and every other weekend, so we still interact, but it's a very transactional interaction. There's no emotion. It's almost like we've become zombies, we don't recognize any humanity in each other anymore. It's kind of like, 'Here, take them, goodbye, see you later,' like just transactional and sometimes I think 'wow, we knew each other for 10 years and now we are just like strangers in the dark.'"

Another man commented, "Uh huh! I know how that is."

The young handsome man continued:

"A lot runs through my brain like, 'How did this happen? How does this happen?' And I'm actually getting to an acceptance place, and I tell myself, 'It happened, deal with it, live with it, you have today to make good decisions, you have today to be a better dad, and you have today and the future to prepare for the future.' I can't keep on going back and beating myself up about things I didn't do or what I should have done and what I could have done differently, and yes there are lessons to learn, but I'm also learning how to let go of the past regrets and all that and be more present. I'm looking forward to the future and trying to be a better person, a better parent, and a better co-parent."

Gatimu began speaking:

"I hear you brother. I've been realizing that I can now reclaim who I used to be when I was single. I used to love doing different things, but over time when I got married, I had to make some compromises. When I became a parent, there are things I stopped doing. I couldn't go hang out with my buddies as much as I wanted to, I couldn't go biking like I used to do when I was still in my teens. I love singing, but I didn't have time to go for choir practice because the kids had to be in bed and all that stuff, so I've been slowly looking back at my life, 15, 20 years ago and asking what did I used to do that used to make me feel alive and full? Can I do it again? So, I've joined a gospel choir, I've been taking dance classes, and I got a mountain bike. I used to mountain bike a lot when I first came to the U.S. and I owned a bike back home in Kenya. I loved the freedom of being on a bike. I also have a road bike that I stopped riding because I didn't have time. I was always at work or running home to help with the kids and even when I tried to ride my bike to work and ride back it would take me much longer to do and my ex-wife would get upset about it, so I started driving. I sacrificed things I love, so I'm reclaiming them again. I've been hanging out with more of my Kenyan friends whom I've missed. One thing I've noticed is Kenyans have a certain way of talking. No offense non-Kenyans in the room...haha! But the way we talk about stuff, like our conversation and our sense of humor, is pretty unique and when I hang out with non-Kenyans, we don't quite attack humor the way we do with just people from Kenya. There are a lot of unspoken things that make us laugh like crazy. I used to do that when I was in grad school with a bunch of Kenyans that were in the Kenyan Students' Association. Even at that time, my ex-wife will tell me that she'd never seen me as happy as when I was in the group, just a bunch of Kenyans laughing about things. I guess it was a reminder of home. I'd laugh until my eyes were tearing up and I rarely do that now. So, it's something else I've been going back to, I've been hanging out with a bunch of Kenyans and just cracking jokes and laughing about stuff."

"Well of course we all think our fellow people have the best sense of humor because we grew up listening to them, so we understand exactly where they are coming from. We know their point of references. I get it Gatimu, keep enjoying your Kenyans, the rest of us will enjoy our own people."

The room felt a little lighter as some people laughed at Gatimu's college friend's comments. The conversation went on for about an hour and a half. Thabiti was amazed at how these men spoke. They were genuinely sharing all their thoughts and feelings about their divorces. Most of them had children as he had, some had been divorced for years while others were more recent. But one thing was certain, they understood how he felt. For the first time since his divorce, he felt seen. Even though he didn't say anything, it was as if he had been talking all night.

When Thabiti lay in his bed that night thinking about this group, something felt different. These men understood what he was going through, and they were choosing to live with the circumstances of their divorce. He was not alone, and just that fact made it bearable for him to face another day.

Chapter References

[14]Fornek, K. (2018, June). Murder-suicide in Darien connected to marital problems, police say. *Chicago Tribune.* Retrieved from https://www.chicagotribune.com/suburbs/burr-ridge/ ct-dbr-darien-murder-suicide-tl-0628-story.html

[15]Mota, C. (2018, May). Days before murder-suicide, man threatened to send wife 'back to Africa in a coffin.' *The Jersey Journal.* Retrieved from https://www.nj.com/hudson/2018/ 05/days_before_murder_man_threat- ened_to_send_wife_bac.html

[18]Nwoye, I. C. (2017, July). The hotline trying to stop men murdering their wives. *Aljazeera.* Retrieved from https://www.aljazeera.com/features/2017/7/21/the-hotline- trying-to-stop-men-murdering-their-wives

[17]Rice, K. (2020, September). Pastor who shot, killed wife threatened to kill her during argument the day before, Orlando police say. *Orlando Sentinel.* Retrieved from https://www.orlandosentinel.com/news/breaking-news/ os-ne-new-details-killing-orlando-pastor-shot- wife-20200912-aqa4cqkoorf7vejly53k7nqxt4-story.html

[16]Sina, K. N. (2020, June). US Homicide : Chris /Annie Takam die in crime of passion. *CRTV.* Retrieved from https://www.crtv.cm/2020/06/us-homicide-chris-annie- takam-die-in-crime-of-passion/

4

Healing After Sexual Assault

Disclaimer: This story contains sensitive information that may be triggering for some.

All Loveline could hear was the panting on the phone as if someone had been running a long distance and stopped to take a break. "Hello, hello, Koloina? What's going on? What's wrong?" Koloina was breathing really hard and it was difficult for Loveline to hear her. "Take a few deep breaths, come on breathe with me... in and out... that's good, that's good. Now talk to me, where are you and what's going on?"

"I'm in..." still trying to catch her breath, "I'm at... you know...," still breathing.

"Koloina, slow down, take your time."

"You know those family friends that I've mentioned before?" Koloina finally got the words out.

"Yes?"

"I'm at their place, in the room," she burst out crying, "I think the dad just tried to have sex with me."

"Oh my goodness! Koloina, are you okay? I'm calling the police. Do you want me to come and get you?"

"Yes please," Koloina was still sobbing.

"What's your address? Are you able to text it to me? Or you can just say it out loud and I'll write it. I'm on my way."

"Loveline, please don't call the police. I'm not ready to deal with all that."

"Ok, I'll be there in about 20 minutes. Lock the door to the room if you can."

Loveline put on her sweater, wore her sneakers, took her car keys and was out the door. She would get there by 12:30am. Angry thoughts raced through her mind as she said a prayer while driving to meet Koloina. They had met about a year ago through their church group and immediately hit it off. Even though Koloina was 19 years old, 11 years younger than her and was the first person she had met from Mauritius, they found that they had a lot in common. Koloina didn't have any family members in the U.S. and was like a little sister to her. Loveline got angry as she thought about what had just happened. The people to whom Koloina's family entrusted her were the people she needed to be protected from. Such a pity. She remembered her aunties and uncles whom her parents connected her with when she came to the U.S., they would never have tried something so despicable. But then, she thought, you just never know.

People can be wolves in sheep's clothing. A tear dropped down Loveline's face as she thought how scary this must be for Koloina with her family being so far away. Fortunately, she was going home next week for the Christmas holidays.

Loveline made it in time and found Koloina standing outside. Parking the car and rushing to her, Loveline asked, "Do you have all your stuff?"

"Yes, I'm ready, let's go."

With her bags safely in the car, they drove off. Koloina was teary-eyed and didn't say much. She looked like she was in shock; almost as if she had drifted off to a different land.

"I'm taking you to my place, okay? You can spend the night and we'll sort things out in the morning."

Koloina nodded.

The only thing Loveline said was, "Whenever you want to talk about it, I'm here."

It was a silent drive home as you could barely hear Richard Bona's album playing in the background.

"Here we are," Loveline broke the silence once they entered through the door to her 2-bedroom apartment.

"Loveline, thank you for believing me. And thanks for coming to get me. I didn't know what to do." Koloina started sobbing again.

Loveline held Koloina and hugged her tight, "I'm sorry this happened to you. It's over." It seemed like a hug that lasted an hour although it was just a few seconds. "I just need to take out a few things from the spare room and then it's all yours." Loveline got the room ready and they both went to bed.

9AM the next day, Saturday

Loveline was sitting at the dining table drinking tea and reading. Thankfully it was a Saturday and she had an open day. As Koloina walked in from her guest bedroom, Loveline said, "Good morning sleepy head. How did you sleep?"

"Surprisingly, I actually got some sleep. It took me a while to fall asleep and I had some weird dreams, but I actually slept well. Your bed is so comfortable." Koloina walked to the kitchen and opened the fridge.

Loveline said, "There's bread, eggs, and some fruit over there. Help yourself to whatever. The tea is in the right cupboard. I'm not so much a coffee person, but there is Ovaltine as well."

"Don't worry, I'll help myself. Bread and eggs sound great, along with some tea. I'm really looking forward to going home next week. It is such perfect timing. What are you doing for the holidays, Loveline?"

"I'll be right here. Laying on my couch and watching Christmas movies. Atem, Sinjuh, Darifa, Lenka, and Loide are coming over for Christmas. We're going to have an African Christmas with food, music, dance, and nonsense talk, you know how we do. Maybe we'll even watch a movie, I don't know, we'll see how it goes."

Koloina soon joined Loveline on the table as they continued talking about their holiday plans.

"I don't know what I'm going to tell my parents when they ask about Uncle Frans."

"Is that your uncle from last night?"

"Yes, but he's not really my uncle. You know how we call older family friends, uncles and aunties? My parents have known their family for years now. I think my dad and he were colleagues from work or so, I can't even remember. With me coming to the U.S., my parents connected us together since they are local. They wanted me to have some familiar faces and some place I can go for breaks and holidays if needed. They've been alright for the past year; I've gone there a few times just to visit. Aunty Minda, his wife sometimes cooks and gives me some to take back with me. She's nice. I just went to spend the weekend because it had been long since I saw them. Aunty Minda always makes those comments of, 'we haven't seen you in a while,' so I decided to go and spend a weekend instead of my usual few hours. When I got there, everything was fine. Close to bedtime Aunty Minda told me she was going to put the kids to bed, so she left. Uncle Frans said he was going to show me my room. He showed me and left. I wasn't intending to sleep right away because I wanted to chat with Aunty Minda. But I guess I was tired, so I just lay my head down and fell asleep on the bed. Next thing I know Uncle Frans was all over me. It was like waking up to a dog licking my face, but he was also touching me all over. It caught me by surprise because I was asleep. When I woke up, I was like, 'Uncle stop!' I think he realized what he was doing and he left the room. While I was still trying to understand what just happened, I heard him and Aunty Minda having sex in the next room. They were so loud that I was like, thank God the kids are upstairs. Loveline, it was horrible. I'm glad that he stopped, but I was still very confused, maybe in shock for the next few minutes. Then, my thoughts started going wild. I think I got myself into a panic attack. I was thinking, 'What if he comes back? They gave me a ride here, where do I go? I can't stay here for the night, not to talk of the weekend. Is what just happened considered sexual assault?' All these thoughts started going through my mind and that's when I decided to call you."

"Koloina, I'm glad you called me. That's such a scary situation to be in. And yes, that is sexual assault. You were sleeping, you didn't give consent, and he touched you sexually. I'm sorry it happened to you. How are you feeling now?"

"I'm still a little shaken. I have a little disbelief because I thought of them as a nice couple and now I don't know what to think. Plus, my parents are going to ask me about them and I don't know what to tell them."

"All that is understandable. Well, you don't have to decide anything right now. You'll figure out what to tell them when the time is right."

"As much as I'm still a little in shock, it's good to be here with you. I feel fortunate that you were available and came and got me immediately."

"Well, sexual abuse is a trigger point for me. Whenever I hear about it, my senses are heightened and I get into protective mode."

"Hmm..." There was a pause for a second. "Why is that Loveline? I mean if you care to share."

"You mean why is it a trigger? Well, where do I begin? It's a long story."

"I'm all ears if you're comfortable with telling me."

"I never told you why my parents separated and why I just started talking to my dad 4 years ago after not speaking to him for 12 years. My dad and I have had a complicated relationship. From the age of 5 to about 13 years old, he molested me.

This was when I was back in Yaoundé in Cameroon. Honestly Koloina, I didn't know there was anything wrong with what he was doing till I was 13 years old. There was this bush faller[19] who used to come to my neighborhood to spend time with one of my neighbors. I'll never forget her. Her name was Anyikeng, but she told us to call her Anyi. She was maybe in her mid-20s at the time but she would come to hang out with my age mate. There was something about her that was very attractive and I don't mean her beauty. She was pretty, but that's not it. And I don't mean money either. If she had money, I couldn't tell. She was simple in appearance, but there was something else about her. She cared about us. She was nice and she actually sat down and talked to us. Most of all, she came to our neighborhood even though she didn't have to. Koloina, I grew up poor. We lived in this slum where we didn't have running water nor stable electricity. We shared a compound with our neighbor. She lived in a one-bedroom house with her mom and brother. They had a few items in their house that I guess you would call furniture. I don't think they really had a bed that was comfortable. They didn't have much going for them and it looked like finances were difficult for them. We were one of the wealthier ones in our neighborhood, we had good enough furniture, a spacious living room, bedrooms with beds, you know. Anyi was Cameroonian by the way, but she was studying in the U.S., her family lived in a different neighborhood in town, that's why I say she didn't have to come to us. She probably had a really nice house, I don't know. She would come to spend time with our neighbor, and they would eat, pray, and study scriptures. They looked like they had fun together. I knew that Anyi and our neighbor went to the same church, and she knew everyone in their family. She would say hi to my mom and I whenever we were around. I was curious about what they were doing, and I wanted to be a part of it. I can't remember if she asked me or if I asked her about doing the Bible studies as well, so she started coming to see me to study the scriptures. My mom knew and she would sometimes sit at the corner while we met. We would sit outside on stools and study. I think our neighbor felt a little jealous when she came to spend time with me as well, but I felt the same way earlier when I saw them together. Now she would spend time with both of us. She showed me different things about God's love for me and how much Jesus sacrificed for me. Those were some of my foundational times in my faith. I was just 13 and I didn't know anything about the Bible. But that's when I started understanding right from wrong. This one day, we were talking about sin and she explained examples of sin. She asked me about my life and what I saw that was sinful. That's when I mentioned sexual immorality and I began to explain what my dad was doing. He used to come into my room and..." Loveline paused for a second.

"I'll spare you the details. Even though it was weird what my dad was doing, I thought it was a special time between my dad and I, like our secret thing. I mean which 5-year-old knows what they are doing? That's what parents are meant for, to guide us... I really appreciate Anyi because she was alarmed, but she didn't cause a scene. She just told me that it was wrong and it was sin. I think she needed time to think about what to do because she called me a few days later and asked if we could meet as a family with her and another woman from her church so that we could talk about what I came to find out later was child molestation.

I remember that meeting like it was yesterday. It was my dad, my mom, Anyi, her friend, and I sitting around the dining table. She started by saying that she had really enjoyed getting to know me and studying the Bible. Then she said there was something that I shared with her that she would like me to share on the table. I was initially scared, but I shared it and this is the part that I can remember very clearly because I was very confused afterward. My dad denied it and kept saying we wanted to spoil his reputation. He started yelling at some point. My mom was stunned and kept asking me, 'why didn't you tell me?'"

I was very confused for a long time after that. My mom took my brother and I and left my dad. Oh and my mom was pregnant at the time. I had mixed feelings about my dad because on the one hand, I loved him and I think I secretly felt jealous of my mom when they were together. My therapist told me my feelings and perceptions were disoriented and I didn't understand what was a right relationship with a father or a man for that matter. I had to learn what appropriate boundaries were. Yes girl, I broke down when I was 22 and went in for therapy. After my mom left him, she never wanted to hear about him, which didn't help me because I missed him but I was also very angry. I was angry at him for molesting me for so many years. I was angry at myself for letting him even though I now know I didn't have control since I was a child. I was angry at my mom for leaving even though I was also glad that she did. And I was angry at Anyi for breaking my family even though she did the right thing. I don't know what else would have been a better approach because at the time in Yaoundé, we didn't have a lot of systems to deal with such cases. Or if we did, I don't think Anyi, her church friend, or my mom knew them. It's the family that resolved issues like this. Call the police for this? They would probably tell him to stop and send her back to him. I sometimes wonder what my life would have looked like if Anyi hadn't intervened at that time. I don't know, but I feel like God used her to expose sin in my family early enough before it destroyed me and my family."

Koloina was listening intently and could only bring herself to say, "Wow Loveline! I had no idea. You seem so strong and self-assured."

"I guess we can't see people's stories written on their faces right? But don't let that fool you, I still have my days. And I have been to therapy, read many books, and prayed a lot. That's the reason why I can even tell this story the way I am telling you right now."

"What ever happened to you and Anyi?" Koloina asked.

"I saw her a few times after that day, but my dad banned us from meeting together immediately after the family meeting. And she went back to the U.S. at some point afterward. We also lost contact because my mom moved. I didn't have a phone number at the time. But I wrote her a letter and sent it through our neighbor, and she replied. I can't even remember what I wrote but I know I had told her that I would never forgive my dad. She told me among other things that I should forgive him and that she was praying for me.

It took me several years to even realize how much the sexual abuse affected me. I still have days where I need to pray and journal through my feelings. I realized that we live in a fallen world and my dad is not immune from sin. The only way I could truly be free is by forgiving him and handing him over to God. Forgiving myself and letting God forgive me for hiding the pain of the abuse. And choosing everyday not to hold his sin against him.

Between the ages of 13 to 22, I didn't talk much about any of this trauma. But I had nightmares and triggers I didn't even notice were triggers. I always felt guilty and ashamed for things I didn't do. I thought there was something wrong with my body, I just always felt unclean and didn't like looking at myself in the mirror. Whenever I watched TV shows or movies where there was any form of sexual harassment or abuse, I would have flashbacks and it would cause me so much anxiety. I experienced PTSD symptoms and didn't realize any of these until my boyfriend in college asked me why I was so weird about my body. I got very angry at him like, 'What do you mean?' He replied, 'Do you even like yourself?' Trust my African people to not know how to be subtle, haha!"

"I know right!"

"But that question did something for me. That's when I started asking more questions about what was going on with me, which began my healing journey."

"That's some journey."

"Yes, it has been. It's not been an easy one."

"If you don't mind me asking, how did you reconcile with your dad?"

"At first, I wasn't planning on talking to him again. I just wanted to forgive and move on, but the more I prayed through it, I felt God was calling me to reach out to him. I think part of the reason is because my dad has changed. From what my aunt, his sister said, he had been trying to connect with me for years. I wasn't ready back then and I'm thankful that my aunt respected that and didn't force me to do anything. Three years ago, I called him. He is still in Cameroon. It was a little strange talking to him, but he was polite and friendly. He apologized for all of it and it even sounded like he got a little emotional on the phone. I didn't know I needed to hear his apology until he said it. I felt like something lifted from my body that I had been carrying for years. I was ready, so I told him right there that I forgave him. The awkward conversation turned into a beautiful one, which opened the door for our relationship. We don't talk frequently, we are still getting to know each other, and I am still building trust, but we have a positive relationship for the most part. I can tell that something happened that changed him and caused him to repent. He sounds different from the person who raised me. My mom on the other hand, still needs to do her own work because she doesn't want me talking to him and she is just an angry person, always yelling. I guess we each have to choose what we do with the trauma that happens in our lives. We can let it control us or we can choose to move forward."

"Hmm!" Koloina sat listening and reflecting on Loveline's story. "You've been on a journey, Loveline. Thanks for sharing your story with me. I wouldn't have been able to tell any of this from knowing you."

"We just don't know what people have been through. Or what they are going through right now."

"Yeah, you're right. We don't."

"All that to say, you'll figure out your own journey."

"I hope so."

"I know so," Loveline said.

Chapter Notes

[19] A slang used in some African countries to describe someone (usually a fellow African) who has traveled abroad.

Resources on Sexual Assault

National Sexual Assault Hotline. RAINN. https://www.rainn.org/

National Sexual Violence Resource Center (NSVRC). https://www.nsvrc.org/survivors

Joyful Heart Foundation http://www.joyfulheartfoundation.org/

NotAlone https://obamawhitehouse.archives.gov/1is2many/notalone

VictimConnect Resource Center https://victimconnect.org/

Sexual Assault Kit Initiative (SAKI) https://www.sakitta.org/survivors/

5

An African Man's Faith

"Most people are lazy; they just want to be told what to think. But you my son, I want you to know HOW to think." Seye remembered his father's words to him when he was still a young boy. He didn't understand it then and he thought his dad was zealous about many topics, especially his faith. Seye would walk into conversations between his father and friends, other times he would hear his name yelled, "Seye!" "Yes Baba!" he would respond. "Come and join the conversation," his dad would say. Seye would come and sit in the living room and watch them go back and forth as they drank palm wine. They spoke about everything and anything, politics, music, history, colonization, tradition, religion, and faith. Books were opened including the Bible and Baba would say, "Seye, read for us." He would direct him to a passage to read and he would tell him where to stop. Seye learned to be an avid reader on many topics, and this is where it all started, as a young boy reading to adults even though he didn't understand half of the things he read.

Seye remembers a conversation they once had about Christianity. He could hear his dad's arguments about the topic:

"Consider Jesus, he rarely gave people the answer, he gave them opportunities to think. He asked people questions, and he told them stories. Where did we get off feeding people religion and asking them to follow along?" His dad would say and some of his friends would nod.

"Consider Paul, even though it can look like he told people what to do, he was actually showing them how to think. You know the problem with church today? We just want to standardize things and make people do them, make them stay in line. We don't want people to think for themselves or God forbid, depend on the Holy Spirit because if they do, we won't like how it will look. We won't be able to tell if they are committed to our congregation or not. The church numbers may look bleak, and you know we want those numbers to be high because we get our egos wrapped up in them. It consoles us to think our churches are growing in number, so we must be doing something right. And we become mixed up thinking when people are in line and the numbers are high, they are doing well spiritually. It didn't faze Jesus that people left him. Didn't he ask his disciples if they wanted to leave?"

Seye didn't remember the responses to his dad's sentiments, but his dad's words still ring clearly to him. Maybe it's because he has been asking some of those questions himself. Or because he always wanted his dad to be proud of him. Either way, those conversations he heard as a young boy were coming up more and more as he grew older. He couldn't remember the answers to many of these questions and he was beginning to think maybe that was part of the point of those discussions, to get each other to think even when they didn't have the answers.

He recalls someone asking, "Is the Proverbs 31 woman actually a woman or does it represent Wisdom? Think about it! Isn't wisdom referred to as a woman in the book of Proverbs? Could the author be telling us more about wisdom than the qualities of a powerful woman?"

The voices would carry on, "Why do you think Okonkwo did what he did to himself? Was it because of his pride? His honor? His refusal to accept a new reality?" Someone else would say, "An African man's pride cannot be tampered with." And another would ask, "What would you have done?"

Seye later got to know that they were talking about "Things Fall Apart" by Chinua Achebe. He thought about the question later on and wasn't sure about his answer to the question, "what would you have done?"

Sometimes the conversations got intense, voices were raised, the mood got somber, or people laughed hysterically. Sometimes his mom would join and give her own opinion, other times she would go to the backyard with some of the aunties and they had their own conversations. Seye didn't know what the women talked about among themselves. But the men and the women talked together frequently so he didn't really think he missed out on much.

Although Seye missed having other children around, after all it was rare to be an only child in his Nigerian household, he didn't feel it that much because his father made sure he was part of almost every conversation. He got used to being the only child in the discussion and he learned quickly how to hold an intelligent conversation.

Seye was now 41 years old, and these conversations came up more frequently in his mind especially the ones about faith. He found that his African friends were on either extreme; one group wanted him to forget about culture and choose Jesus and the other group wanted him to choose culture and let go of the concept of one God. Why couldn't he have both?

In a conversation, one of his friends said to him, "I think about things that indigenous Africans have, our culture, our religion, our spirituality that were kind of pushed aside by Europeans and you know I don't quite subscribe to the idea that there's only one way to heaven and there's only one religion and all. Our cultural and religious stuff was real. Our people developed that stuff, and it was only a matter of who had the gun that changed the way things worked. I think it's still valid what our grandparents and great-grandparents and all the ancestors had. They are ideals I still like and value. If someone tries to push a monotheistic view of the world like, 'yeah I don't know why you guys have polygamy, that's wrong' and stuff like that, those are things that kind of turn me off."

Seye didn't necessarily agree with his friend's views, and he thought he needed to get some of his facts right. But he understood his friend's desire to validate what had been invalidated through colonization and centuries of denigrating Africans.

He also knew through his research that Christianity had been in Africa long before colonization. It was a consolation to learn that God had not forgotten about them. God had not brought

Christ only through suffering and the deceit of colonial masters. Rather Jesus was thinking about them on the journey to the cross as Simon of Cyrene, an African, helped him carry the cross.

God was intentional about having the city, Cyrene, mentioned in the scriptures. He wanted people everywhere to know that Simon was from Cyrene, a place that can be traced back to North Africa, which is today's Libya. And then there is the rich Christian history in Ethiopia. The Ethiopian eunuch believed and got baptized in the book of Acts. There were multiple other early disciples that can be traced back to Africa. Seye had some answers, but he had more questions.

"If I could believe in Jesus, there's hope for anyone," his father had told him. Seye had always known his father as a Christian, but apparently that wasn't always the case. His father was a very traditional man; he cared about his African traditions. His ancestry was extremely important, and he believed his ancestors had a lot of wisdom. So, for anyone to tell him he needed to forget all of that in order to become a Christian was an abomination. Nonetheless, something changed that made him appreciate both his traditions and his faith. Seye didn't care about this when he was younger, but within the past few years, he wondered, "How did Baba accept both?"

Living in the U.S. now for 20 years, he was already getting far removed from his African traditions. He saw his faith being Westernized as he tried to separate faith from culture. "What is my Biblical faith and what is my cultural conditioning?" Seye grappled with this question and whenever he brought it up to his friends and even his pastor, they were downplayed with phrases like, "What does it matter? Jesus is Lord, right?" or "We'll get to that question later, I'm concerned about your walk with God." Seye left many conversations frustrated because he felt his questions were unquestionable. Why were Christians more concerned about their agenda with people than God's agenda with people? Was God not big enough to answer his questions? Why were people treating him as if he had lost his faith when he was wrestling with God? Was it so wrong for him to wonder about his ancestors and if they were going to heaven?

Seye thought of his mother's words. She would say to him, "Don't worry about the future, Jesus will be there with you." It didn't feel that way. Actually, it seemed his questions were falling on the ground and being trampled upon. He felt alone. Has anyone struggled like he was and still called themselves Christian? Was he losing his faith? As he drifted asleep, his mind still thinking of multiple questions, he heard a whisper, "Baba would know." Seye almost missed it, but then it dawned on him, "Yes Baba would know." His father had had similar questions. Why didn't he think of talking to him earlier? It was a 6-hour time difference between Texas and Lagos. He would have to wait till tomorrow to call home. Seye rolled in his bed and was finally able to go to sleep, "tomorrow" he thought.

Sunday 12pm Texas time, 6pm Lagos time

The next afternoon, Seye was glad to get his parents on the phone...

"Yes Mama, you know I'm a grown man now, right?" Seye was telling his mom on the phone as she went on about if he was eating well and doing other normal things that humans do. "African parents just can't help themselves no matter how old you are," he thought. "Here is your father," she said as she gave the phone to his father. After a few minutes of banter back and forth, Seye asked, "Baba, can I ask you something?"

"Anything, my son."

"Do you remember the time you told me that if you could become a Christian, there was hope for anyone?"

"Uh huh"

He pictured his dad nodding. "Tell me more about that. What made it difficult for you?"

"Well ehm..." Seye's dad reflected out loud, "Being the oldest of 10 children in my father's house, I had a lot of responsibilities. Some were to my siblings, and some were to my tradition. I felt it was my duty to maintain my roots. Christianity, the way it was initially presented to me, wanted to rid me of my culture. However, I learned the truth when I fully understood. Jesus was from the East not the West and he was Jewish. He respected and participated in his cultural traditions, but these traditions never took precedence over his Father's will. It was always God over everything."

"Hmm Papa, I hear you. But how did you reconcile the two? Your African culture and your Christianity?"

"Your question is implying that they are in conflict. Are they? Doesn't every society have a culture?"

"Yes, but it is my perception that my culture has constantly been shunned as not Christian enough. I wonder if people are being converted to follow Christ or to Westernized Christianity."

"I hear you, I hear you. As a matter of fact, these were some of my own questions in my early years and I saw, still see many

African men shut off because of these concerns for fear that their African identity will be stripped away. This is what we do as men. We make sure bad things never happen again or at least we try. African men have been dehumanized throughout history. They have been made to look strong yet feel weak. As a result, they harden up so that they don't feel those things again or they try to control their families so they can get a semblance of order. It makes them feel like they are managing their lives, but all the while they are inwardly crushed refusing to think too hard about difficult questions for fear that they won't like the answers. Or God forbid, the answers would require them to change. Instead, they go along with their work day-in and day-out, building castles in the air and trying not to look down so they don't fall. But you, Seye, you are not afraid to ask the hard questions. You are not afraid to look for the answers. I taught you well *sha*... they say like father like son, you are definitely my son."

Seye felt a flush of embarrassment, yet he was glad that his father was proud of him for the questions that many others had made him feel ashamed to ask.

His father went on, "We tell people to wrestle with God, but we really don't want them to wrestle too hard or for too long because when they do, we tell them to get it together or we look at them like they have lost their faith. Sometimes we can't explain what's happening to people. Even the scriptures say, *The wind blows wherever it pleases. You hear its sound, but you cannot tell where it comes from or where it is going. So it is with everyone born of the Spirit*[20]. We can't always understand the work of the Spirit. And that scares us. Doesn't wrestling mean asking difficult questions and allowing God to take you on the journey to find the answers? To learn to trust him regardless of the answers? That type of wrestling takes time and that's something we don't like to give people or ourselves. Not many people give themselves enough time to get the answers. They cut the process prematurely because they are afraid of where God will take them to find the answers. They fear that they may lose themselves. But isn't that the whole point, to lose yourself for God's sake so that you may truly find life in Him? We want answers now, give it to me short and sweet. Well, my son, God is patient, and He has time. We can make time too."

Seye was a little relieved upon hearing his father. He felt affirmed and challenged at the same time, thinking through what all of this meant for him in this season of his life. Where was God taking him and was he willing to go there? Interrupting his thoughts, his father spoke again:

"These are the tensions we carry; how do we accept a religion that was used to drag us into slavery and colonization, and neo-colonization for that matter? How do we contend with a God who allowed all of it to happen? What about our ancestors and what they practiced? And I add, how does a God as mighty and powerful as He even allow us to question Him? All by His love and mercy. Does man's wickedness through all generations erase God's goodness? He gave us freewill, didn't He? Freewill means giving us the choice of good or evil *abi*? We want Him to stop the bad but not the good. We want Him to interfere in our free-will when we think it will not serve us, but not when it will give us what we want in the moment. At what point does His interference take away our freewill? Will that be acting in love anymore? Think about it. If a loving Father gives you freedom to do whatever you want and then starts interfering in your decisions, wouldn't you be angry at Him for going against Himself? 'Ah ah you said you will let me choose. Why are you trying to choose for me?'"

Seye chuckled a little as he listened intently to his father's words.

"We want to blame God for the wickedness of man when those are the choices we made with our freewill..."

There was a pause for a few seconds before his father resumed talking almost switching topic to answer the question about ancestors:

"Doesn't God judge us based on what we know, not what we don't know? Abraham didn't know Jesus but he was made righteous by his faith right? God saw his heart just like He saw all the other people's hearts in the Bible. Seye, you know this is not new; the story of our ancestors is not new. Throughout the Bible there were people worshiping various mini-gods and doing various practices while others worshiped the one true God. How did God deal with them? You've read it right? You know what I'm talking about. God knew who his true followers were. Hebrews 11 tells us a few of them. For our ancestors, God knows and He will judge each one accordingly. For us, we know Jesus today. There is enough evidence to show that he is the son of God and God himself in the flesh. God will judge us accordingly. God meets each of us where we are with what he has revealed in time. He hadn't revealed Jesus then, but he has revealed him now."

"Hmm..." was the only sound that came out from Seye.

"Seye, you may not get all the answers you seek. Actually, I don't have all my answers. But that doesn't mean you shouldn't ask the questions. It is in the asking that we connect with God and with people, this is part of our journey with God. He may not respond in the ways you expect, but He helps you to be okay with the answers you get. He even helps you to be okay with the unanswered questions. Look at Job, he didn't get the answers to his questions for why he suffered, but he learned other things about the God he served. God helps you to trust Him alone. This is faith! And you know we live by faith not by sight."

Seye was silent as he took in his father's words. The father and son had more exchanges. Then, as if his father was giving a final warning, he said:

"By the way, Seye, God created you and I as thinkers. I'm sure you already know that. As someone who God created to be a thinker, my faith has shifted several times throughout my life. I've come to understand this shifting as God taking me into new territory. It might initially feel strange, even as if I am drifting away, but no my son, He's always drawing me closer to Him. People may not understand it and I don't think they need to because God does. He knows. Don't be afraid to get into new territory with God. Even though the process can be excruciating, the outcome is always good. God will never fail. You may come out with deeper love, deeper understanding, more wisdom, and deeper commitment to the One who sees you. Just stay close to Him. You can't wrestle with God without wrestling with His Word, read it! And pray constantly. He is the only one who can truly get you there. You may be tempted to avoid by getting busier at work or in house repairs, but don't give in to that. You may be tempted to isolate as if nobody in the world can under-stand you, but don't fall for that either. Why do you think your mother and I had those uncles and aunties here to discuss? And that we invited you to join? That was our way of wrestling with people we knew could talk about these issues. We wanted you to learn how to think and learn how to do it with others."

"Baba, I hear you. But you know life in the U.S. is not like life back home. It is difficult to find that."

"I know I know Seye! And even though we all can think, many people don't want to think. Trust me, even though there are people in and out of this house visiting and chatting with us, if you notice, we don't have the same conversations with all of them. We didn't meet our wrestling thinkers overnight. It took years and prayers. Your mother and I were intentional about this. Pray and ask God to send you your people. But until then, I am here as long as I am alive to wrestle with you."

Seye felt a huge weight lifted as he and his father continued their conversation. Although all his questions weren't answered, he felt an influx of hope. He was grateful to be called this man's son.

Chapter Notes
[20] John 3:8

6

Lost In Migration

"Ah dey fine, Big Mami. How for you?" [21]

"Ah dey fine too. How for school[22]?"

"School di waka fine. Ah di kam graduate small time.[23]"

"Oh that's good. That's good. You stay fine[24] eh!"

"Yes, thank you Big Mami. You too, take care."

And that's how our exchanges usually went. From all I knew through my mother and aunts about my Big Mami, what you just read is all my Big Mami and I could actually exchange with each other.

I know that Big Mami lived in Fontem where she grew up and married her husband of over 40 years. She knew almost every corner of Fontem. She understood the way of life, she spoke the language everyone spoke there, she knew the good days to go to the market, and she knew what particular vendors she was going to buy from. She owned her own farm where she grew the foods she enjoyed to cook and eat. She sold some and made a profit for herself. She had friends and neighbors who knew her, they exchanged stories of good times and bad times. They even watered her farm when she went to the city to visit her son and his family. She understood her environment, her culture, and the people. Her life was full even after her husband passed away 5 years before she came to America. Mami said it was hard for her because they were married for so long, but she had family and friends all around her, so her life was manageable. Big Mami always kept herself busy doing things she knew how to do. In today's world, we would call her an entrepreneur. She was resourceful and quite generous with what she made.

When we spoke, I always felt a lingering sense of wanting more and I could tell she wanted more too, but our language barriers wouldn't permit us.

Maybe I was too proud to try harder to speak Nweh, the language she knew fluently or maybe I should blame it on my parents. They both spoke fluent Nweh but didn't think it was important to teach us until we were grown and out of the house. In hindsight, we all have regrets; they wish they taught us, and I wish I were more interested in learning the language. I don't blame them; I blame the colonizers. This is one of the effects of colonization. But then, we can keep going further and further, blaming whoever or whatever circumstances. What is all the blame going to do now? Nothing. Here we are! We can't go back; we can only work with what we have right now.

I am an adult born and raised in the motherland who doesn't know how to speak her mother tongue. I only know the colonizers' languages. It has its benefits, but it definitely has its disadvantages and one that I often think about is the generational relationships lost.

I'm sure you figured I'm talking about the relationship between a grandmother and her grandchild, that is my relationship with my grandmother.

Don't we all love those stories of the grandchild sitting on her grandmother's lap listening to old folk tales? It looks nice in the movies, heck it looks nice when I see African American grand mothers and their grandchildren. They pass down love, wisdom, and tell stories just the way only they can do. I feel a little envious because I don't experience that, not because my Big Mami doesn't love me and not because she isn't alive. But because we don't speak the same language. Our exchanges are short and brief.

I used to tug at my mom's African wrapper asking her, "What did Big Mami say?" They will laugh out loud in conversation, and I will look around asking, "What did they say?" "Can someone translate please? I want to be a part of the conversation."

"If it bothers you so much, why don't you just learn the language then?" You ask.

It's complicated. Let me give you some context. As you might know, Africa was made up of multiple states and empires before European colonization from the late 1800s to late 1900s. Each of these African regions had tribes with different languages and customs. Some languages were written but many were passed on orally from generation to generation. My native language called Nweh was one of the oral ones. After regaining independence from Europeans who split Africa into today's present countries, many African people were left speaking the European languages. It makes sense as European masters established schools to teach in their languages and methods. Plus, many Africans were left to believe that their customs and languages were primitive, so they needed to aspire for European ideals.

Bear in mind that many African countries just regained independence in the 1960s. That's within my parents' lifetime, a little over 60 years ago. This was not long ago. Wow! This was really not long ago. If I could have conversations with my grandmother, she would probably have stories to tell me about that time.

So, what happened after independence from colonial masters? Migration happened. Many people moved out of the rural areas to the industrialized cities. Some people moved out of Africa to the Western world to further the education the Europeans had promoted in Africa, while others stayed in the rural areas. All the migration contributed further to the differences in ideals, languages, and cultures between individuals from the same region, even from the same family.

I'm sure you can see how that is the same thing happening now worldwide with globalization. Yes, there is much that we gain from migration, but some things are lost. Among many, the close family ties are threatened especially for people like us, Africans who are communal people. How do we maintain family closeness when we live in various cities, countries, continents, and we don't speak the same language nor have the same customs? You see what I mean?

So, going back to your question of why don't I just learn the language? I know I'm beating around the bush to answer your question, but I just want to help you understand how we got here in the first place. Let me explain how the whole Africa-Europe colonial past affects us on a familial level.

My grandparents chose to remain in the rural areas where they grew up and had their way of living which was more tied to the traditional customs. My parents chose to move to the industrialized cities which had a good mixture of traditional customs and European influence. My parents had a good influence of both. They spoke their native tongue, Nweh, and they spoke their colonial masters' languages English and French. When they began raising children, they were told by colonial educators that teaching their children the native language was going to interfere with their educational development, making it more difficult for them to learn.

Who knows if this was their way of enforcing their own languages and downplaying the African native language. Or maybe the colonial teachers were ignorant themselves about language development because research today tells us that the best time to teach your children multiple languages is as early as possible. The young brain is so malleable to learning that they easily adopt and recreate pronunciations.[25]

The long story short is that my parents thought they were doing what was best by raising their children to primarily speak English and French. Now you understand why I don't speak the language. Moreover, when you grow up in a city like I did, you leave your region of origin where the primary language spoken is your native tongue. You join a community of people from various regions, so you learn the dominant languages, which back then were English and French. Now you know.

To make matters worse, I moved to America, even further removed from my homeland. So just to summarize the generational gap again: my grandparents live in a rural area, my parents live in an industrialized city, I live outside of the country in a Western continent.

They say the best way to learn a language is to live in an environment where that language is spoken. Well, that would mean me living in Muabete or Fontem or Fuatabong, not living in Atlanta, GA. Who is going to speak Nweh with me here? I didn't learn when I was home with close family who spoke it, you think I am going to learn it here when I don't live with them anymore? When I don't have books written in the language, and it is not needed in my daily functioning? I don't think so.

So why don't I just learn the language? Because I have other things to worry about. You know how life is. I mean yes, I can set up a time each week with my parents and ask them to teach me. Or I can call home to speak to other relatives and ask them to teach me. But when I call home, I just want to talk, I don't want to be taught. And how frequently do I talk to my parents for that to be a good use of our time when we both speak English? Why even bother?

But sometimes I think about all the grandmothers with whom I have had closer relationships than my own Big Mami. Something makes me wonder if my relationship with my Big Mami would have been any different if we spoke the same language. I mean I have many relatives with whom I'm not close even though we speak the same language. So, would it really be what

I dream it will be? They say relationships are what you make of them. If you work at it, it will grow. Maybe I don't really want it although I'm here crying to you about it.

Well, guess what? I have another chance to connect with my Big Mami and to maybe even learn Nweh. How? People have started writing books and doing videos to translate Nweh to English. Isn't that wonderful? It is, right? Right! That's just the beginning.

My second chance is that my Big Mami is coming to America. When we spoke on the phone, well you already know how our brief exchanges go, I heard some excitement in her voice. I mean, the famous America, who doesn't want to come here, right? Plus, she is going to see more of her family.

She will be helping to care for her grand babies, my cousins and great grand babies, my nephew and niece. You know this is common for many of our African grandmothers to come to America and help with child rearing. Big Mami is going to stay with my aunt (my mother's sister, Aunty Mafua) and her family. So, my goal immediately after I found out, was to plan to visit as frequently as possible.

I had already planned to spend more time with my baby cousins especially because they live close enough. By the way, that's another issue we face. Back home, people live so nearby, it's easy for us to visit each other as frequently as we want unannounced. But here in America, life is so busy, and distances are so far away. You have to buy an air ticket to go see family, and then plan to be back by Sunday so you can return to work on Monday. It gets exhausting especially in a country where we have all been trained to live to work. Thankfully, my aunt lives close enough, so I just have to drive for an hour to see her, my uncle, and cousins. I am excited about getting to see my Big Mami often as well.

Before my Big Mami migrated, I often wondered how she felt watching generations of her family grow and change and not being able to pass on the wisdom she so desperately wanted to pass on to them. If she sometimes feels like there is a volcano inside of her watching and waiting to erupt but constantly having to calm itself down. Growing old must be a strange thing. It's felt that way for me and I'm still young, only in my 20s. It must be strange witnessing all the changes in the world. It must be strange being surrounded by youngsters, feeling like yourself but watching your body change, not being able to move and walk the way you used to. It must be strange opening your mouth to speak and noticing that your voice sounds a little different. You speak a little slower, and sometimes you can't communicate with all these young people around you because they don't understand your language.

Until my Big Mami migrated, I hadn't really thought about aging in a different culture. People say they feel differently when they speak their mother tongue. They almost become a new person when they learn a new language and live in a new environment. I wondered if this was happening with my Big Mami because she sounded excited to move to the U.S. initially. She was going to be with family she hadn't seen in years. She was coming to America, the land of opportunity. She had a reason to be here, to care for her grand babies and to be with her family. However, she seemed more solemn now that she had been in the

U.S. for a few months. I couldn't help but wonder what she had to give up to be here.

Well, she moved to Lithonia, GA and her sole job was to be with her daughter's family and help with the kids. She had no friends here, did not speak the language, did not understand the culture, and did not know her way around. She never needed to drive anywhere back in Fontem, but here she needed to be driven to go to the nearest grocery store. She couldn't do much on her own. Even the food was different. Yes, my aunt, her daughter often went to an African market to get food similar to what they ate back home, but it was nothing compared to the plethora of dishes Big Mami was used to making from her farm. I watched Big Mami adjust or try to at least. Being that I couldn't exchange much with her in words, we communicated through a lot of facial expressions and hand gestures as I mouthed words in English and she did the same in Nweh. She loved her grand babies and she took good care of them. My aunt would have been a mess without her. But I sometimes noticed her sitting with her hand supporting her head as she daydreamed. I wondered what she thought about. Was she dreaming about her farm, about her friends, about the life she had left behind, or about what she was doing here?

"Aunty ask Big Mami what she is thinking about," I would tell my aunt. "How do you say, 'Big Mami, what are you thinking about in Nweh?'"

My aunt asked her. My Big Mami giggled then spoke a few words, which my aunt translated to me as:

"I'm thinking about Big Papa. I wonder if he would have liked America."

She paused then she continued saying something else which my aunt said was:

"I'm also thinking of starting a farm behind the house here. Maybe you can help me get some seeds."

My aunt responded saying it was a good idea and proposed that they consult with a fellow relative who had a thriving garden behind her house. She nominated me to do research on local crops that may be of interest to Big Mami. I thought Big Mami was done, but she had more to say, which my aunt translated as:

"I'm also thinking I want to knit some sweaters for the kids. If I sit idly a little longer, I will drive myself crazy."

At this, she burst out laughing and my aunt joined her in laughter and whispered to me, "Sounds like my mother. She wants to knit sweaters for the kids; she has always known how to keep herself busy, doing something with her hands."

Aunty Mafua and Big Mami exchanged a few other words and laughed as they spoke.

Big Mami had not lost her entrepreneurial spirit. I walked away recognizing how resilient she was. While I was thinking of all the things she had given up to be here, she was thinking of all the opportunities she had here to make something new. She was right. Yes, there are things that have been lost. But there are also new opportunities to create something in her new environment. Big Mami is a great example of someone who knows the talents she has and uses them to the best of her ability regardless of where she is.

Now I know why my mom used to say I remind her of Big Mami, always looking for the next opportunity to do something creative. I guess that's why they say, "Like mother like daughter" or in this case, "Like grandmother like granddaughter."

Chapter Notes

[21] In Cameroonian pidgin English meaning, "I'm fine, grandmom. How are you?"

[22] In Cameroonian pidgin English meaning, "I'm fine as well. How is school going?"

[23] In Cameroonian pidgin English meaning, "School is going well. I will be graduating soon."

[24] In Cameroonian pidgin English meaning, "Be well."

[25] Liberman, Z., Woodward, A. L., Keysar, B., & Kinzler, K. D. (2017). Exposure to multiple languages enhances communication skills in infancy. Developmental science, 20(1), e12420.

7

Losing A Loved One

Disclaimer: This story contains sensitive information that may be triggering for some.

Papina was interrupted by the door creaking open. Adamou and Ramatou walked in to meet the other four friends in the room. They were sitting in a circle as they usually did; six friends talking about the losses of their loved ones.

Papina, the skeptical one, is a Ghanaian woman in her mid-30s who lost her sister unexpectedly.

Adamou and Ramatou, the faithful ones, are a couple in their 50s from Chad. They are Christian converts who are wrestling with the loss of their son.

Ozigbodi, the strong one, is a Ghanaian woman in her late 30s who lost her husband unexpectedly.

Fifi, the bubbly one, is a woman in her 40s from the Democratic Republic of Congo who lost her dad.

Cederic, the quiet one from Côte d'Ivoire is in his mid-40s. He lost his mother. He is the one who sparked the idea of a group of friends working through their grief together. Today, he has been tasked to read the questions given by Leke, who is the one missing.

Leke, the sensitive one, is a Cameroonian man in his late 30s who also lost his mother. He is a professional counselor who decided to collaborate with his friend Cederic to help in this process of grieving with friends.

"Sorry we're late, we had to drop off the kids at home with their grandma before rushing here," Adamou said apologetically. "Papina please continue."

"It's okay, I just started talking. The question we're answering is, how has the loss impacted you?"

"Ah ok!" Adamou exclaimed as he and Ramatou sat down joining the others.

Papina continued:

"My sister's death was so sudden that it really affected me. I would say it changed my life. You knew this person was a part of your life. I had all these visions about her coming here to join us and all the things we were going to do together and then just one day, she wasn't there. So, it was really hard. And then like I said, she was the one person that I felt really comfortable talking about everything from my kids to my marriage, to school life, everything. We would talk about life here as an immigrant in America, we would laugh. I don't have that in anybody else except you all now. I've gone through lots of emotions, I've been depressed. The grieving process has taken much longer, I guess because it was so sudden. For a very long time, I was still in shock. It was just hard for me to imagine her being dead. I felt like it's not real, how can she be dead? For almost a year, that's the space I was in, and it was really hard for me to get out of it. But, gradually I'm getting better..."

There was a moment of silence, but they were used to it by now. Although he couldn't be here today, Leke had prepared them not to be afraid of the silence. He said it gave people the opportunity to reflect and sit with their emotions.

"Most people rush through life especially in the U.S. without noticing their feelings or the tension in their bodies. The way of life back home in Africa is different; the pace is slower, people are not in a hurry all the time, and it is a lot more communal. Here in the U.S., life is busy, people are always on the move, and it is more individualistic. These aspects affect the grieving process. After the first month or two, people forget that you are still grieving, they move on and you are left with your pain, your loss, your thoughts, and in some cases, the belongings of the person who is gone," Leke told them. Being with this group of friends was their time to slow down, think about the loss, and get in touch with their feelings.

Ozigbodi broke the silence, "I mean losing someone is ehm..." she paused and took a deep breath before continuing:

"I've lost family members, but it wasn't really close to home. Losing a spouse is completely different. No one else's situation is the same so it's difficult especially considering how happy I was in my relationship and that we are still in our 30s. It's that feeling of being empty, lonely, not having the person there all the time you know, it's a hard transition. But it takes time and a lot of thinking." She paused again for a few seconds...

Seeing Ozigbodi's gaze, Fifi spoke trying to help her say more, "It's like your whole world is changed..."

Ozigbodi continued, "Yes and starting over..." she shook her head. "Sometimes you don't know where to start because it takes you a while, you know, and that's why I go back to remembering how happy I was and how long I was in the relationship. All those are factors that play into losing someone. It is more difficult if it's sudden like mine. This was very sudden, so unexpected."

She slowed down her words and mumbled in a quiet voice as she gazed at a spot on the floor:

"It makes it very hard... makes it very hard... and you keep playing it over and over in your head. Why? Why? You keep asking yourself, why did this happen?"

She paused for a second before interrupting her process:

"But having a strong belief in God helps you to re-center yourself and try to move forward because you just have to try each and every day."

The group was used to Ozigbodi holding it in, trying to be strong even though they could tell there was an ocean of tears welling up inside of her. They had come to understand that each person dealt with their grief differently. So, they were patient and willing to provide a safe haven whenever she was ready for her emotions to erupt.

Fifi said:

"When my father passed away, it was very hard. You feel like someone who has been protecting you is no longer there. You feel like you are alone. No matter how old I am, I still miss him. I still think about his stories, his euh, how do you say 'mises en garde?' euh euh!" She thought for a few seconds before saying:

"The way he would warn us about things. Even the things that used to anger me about him, I miss them. I miss how he used to shout whenever he spoke on the phone. My brothers and I would tell him, 'on t'entend' 'we can hear you, even the neighbors can hear you.'" She chuckled before continuing.

"When I moved to the States from the DRC, whenever I would call him, he would ask me, 'Fifi, tu manges quoi aujourd'hui?' I didn't think much about why he kept asking me what I'm eating today. But after he passed, I thought about it. Maybe he wanted to know if my eating changed since I came to America, or he wanted to know if I still eat my traditional dishes. Or maybe he wanted to understand what type of food Africans in America eat or maybe he wanted to know that I was taking care of myself and eating well. I don't know. I just used to answer him and explain everything I was eating. That was one thing we always talked about, food. I miss that too. I miss that question. I miss talking to him."

"It's interesting right? Our parents always want to take care of us no matter how old we get." Adamou said, then he continued:

"You bring your children into this world and pray that God will keep them safe and take care of them. We pray that God will help us to be good parents, that our children will make the right choices and grow up to be decent human beings." He paused for a second, then continued:

"So many hopes and dreams we have for our children. Life doesn't prepare you for when a child decides to take his own life."

He paused and almost choked on his own spit before continuing:

"I've asked myself all kinds of questions, all types of questions like what did I do wrong? I mean he had a bright future in front of him. He is young... was... was... he is a was. That is hard to say... he was smart, he was a funny boy that one. I just didn't see it coming, I didn't see it at all. What was I so busy doing that I didn't notice? I should have paid more attention. But would that have stopped him? I know that we can't go back, but oh how many times I have replayed the scenarios in my head. We should not have come to America at all, I didn't hear much about suicide back home. We should have sent him to a boarding school back home, that's where I went to school. I should have spent more time with him. I should have, I should have, I should have, I should have..." Adamou started sobbing leaning over with his face in his palms.

Tears welled up in Ramatou's eyes as she moved closer to her husband and rubbed his back. Cederic reached out his hand and placed it on Adamou's left shoulder. Ozigbodi began crying as well, unsure if her tears were for him or herself. It didn't matter, there were tears to be cried, this was her chance to let them out. Nobody said a word for as long as they cried.

Leke had told them, "Practice being silent. Many of our parents said to us, 'don't cry, stop crying.' They even made a whole song about it, 'Bébé ohoh don't cry oh,' they used to sing it to us as kids. That is not what we are doing here. This is a place where it is good to cry. Crying at the funeral is just the beginning of all the tears that I encourage you to continue to cry as you mourn your loss. When someone cries, cry with them, sit with them, touch them, allow the space for them to cry. You don't have to say anything. It will feel very uncomfortable in the beginning, but you will get used to it. Let it happen."

So, they sat and cried and then Adamou spoke again:

"I see Ramatou and our other two children suffering. I don't know what to say to them, I don't know what to do for them, I don't even know how to help myself. Life doesn't just stop to let you catch a breath. I know my boss has said take all the time you need, but how much time is that? Can you put a clock on how long it will take for me to get over my son not being here and that he chose to take his own life? And who is going to provide for my family if I take too much time off? What do I do if I am not working? What do I do with myself? Sometimes I feel like I am drowning, and I ask myself, 'Is this life? Is this my life?' Could it get any worse than this? God, how do I handle this?"

Still rubbing her husband's back, Ramatou said:

"We can only do what we can do, the rest is in God's hands. I have asked myself many of the same questions and more. But you know what? Only God knows what our son was going through. We cannot control what our children choose to do. It is not our fault. Adamou, it is not your fault. We prayed. And we will continue to pray for God to help us, for God to help the children. We were trying the best that we knew how. Only God knows. God sees. It shall be well. We shall be well. The children will be okay. We will get through this. We cannot live in this place of questions. It will almost be a year you know. At some point, we have to accept that this is a part of our lives, a very dark part, but a part of it regardless. God will see us through."

The room was silent for a short while, then Amadou spoke up, "You're right. We will trust God and continue to carry on."

He wiped his tears and began to sit up straight before saying:

"Each time Ramatou and I talk about our loss, it is almost as if we take over the whole room. I thank God that Leke reminded us that each of our losses are significant. There is no one that is too small or too big. Your problem is your problem. You only have your life to live and so who am I to compare my problems with yours? Your portion is your portion that God allowed in your life. Ramatou and I want to continue to honor each person's struggle."

Adamou felt the need to say this maybe because of the heaviness he felt in the room, or maybe it was his own discomfort with talking so vulnerably about his feelings about losing his son.

"Thanks for saying that Adamou. I can imagine it is not easy for any of us in this room, that's why we are here," Cederic responded. "We are all getting through our grief together. Should we go to the next question?"

Looking around the room and seeing most people nod in agreement, Cederic asked the next question:

"What has gotten you through thus far? In other words what has helped you get through the loss?"

As usual, Leke had written out 5 questions for the group of 7 people to answer. Although Leke was a trained counselor, he had expressed to them that he wasn't playing the role of a counselor in this group. Rather, he was among friends, and he also needed the group to share his own struggles with losing his mother 6 months ago. Nevertheless, during the first meeting, Leke provided some psychoeducation on how to foster sharing and emotional expression during their time together. He often provided reminders along the way and those present appreciated his insight. Being that he couldn't be here today, he handed over the questions to Cederic to read.

Ozigbodi began to answer the question:

"It is a cultural thing in many parts of Africa where immediately somebody passes, family members or people will come and sympathize with you at your home. They will bring food and drink for days. They will sit with you. They will organize gatherings just to cry with you. You just hear people wailing and wailing in the house. It is like some type of catharsis getting it out. While here in the U.S., sometimes it seems other people feel like, 'oh let's give her space, you know, let's give her space until she's ready' but then in our culture we want to be there right away to support. So, it was nice having people around when my husband died. It was nice having people around, you know, people were coming in and out daily to support me.

In Ghana, they have a bunch of traditional things that they do, like they celebrate the one week after the person dies so that they can get more information on what is happening. This celebration is also to get the program for the date for burial. Typically, the one-week celebration is for family members only. People feel like they need to be there to, you know, to be part of the planning process, so they know what is happening and can provide any support that they can. Then the other part is people are there to provide you with food and all that because they know that you have guests. But, here in the US, it can be very isolating sometimes. Thankfully, I have a strong faith in God so usually that would be my first place to go because the Bible is there. It has a lot of answers for every situation and then you can apply it to your life. So that would be my first resource to use.

I also do a lot of talking to loved ones, friends, brainstorming, reading a lot of books to understand if somebody else has experienced this before to make sense of it. Having a family that supports me has definitely helped but it is harder since family is far away. Living in the states, I can say I have friends, I have co-workers that understand, and I have people who are willing to support me, it helps.

I know sometimes they say go back to work. Hopefully being in the environment and seeing the people you work with will help. But when you are home and you don't have anyone to support you or when you call on someone you know and no one answers, it takes your mind back to the loss. If he was here, this wouldn't have been happening to you or you would have that support system, but now you have to go find support systems elsewhere. You also have to think about if it is really genuine, you know. But keeping the faith as I said, keeping the faith in God and trusting that He will see you through this time."

"I hear you Ozigbodi," Fifi said. "Back in DRC, we cry aloud but people in the States don't cry. We let our emotions out by crying, we cry loud and then after that, we feel good and so yah. My 9 siblings and I have a Whatsapp group that is only us. Our children have their own, but we have one for only my 2 sisters, my 7 brothers, and I. That's where I go. You vent, if you feel like crying, you say, 'guys, I feel like this,' you know. So, I thank God for technology. Talking to my brothers and sisters, knowing that they share the same feelings I do, you know, that helps. We trust each other, we are very close, we love each other.

I can't even think my brother or sister will talk behind my back, no, talk against me, no. We are just very close so for me, besides my husband, I think my family has my back.

Praying, listening to music, and us Congolese, we love to dance. I dance even when there is no music. I pray a lot, I listen to music, and I dance. I also have a very good relationship with my husband and that has helped a lot."

Papina spoke:

"I've been through stuff, and I've considered a lot of things. One of the things that has seen me through is of course my faith because I'm a strong Christian. Even though I still don't understand why she had to go the way she did, my faith has just... I'll say it's been the single thing that has helped me through. I've considered so many things. I've considered going to counseling, but it's a whole bunch of issues. I don't trust any counselor to even understand what I'm feeling. You know, multiple times I've come so close to even scheduling appointments. I've even made some calls to go to counseling and then I'm like 'forget it.' I've prayed, I've cried, I've done everything.

I'm glad that Cederic asked us to meet together like this because it has really changed my life. I feel like I have friends who understand me. It has made me also realize that maybe counseling is not that bad, even though I know this is a little different because it is a group among friends."

"Oh! I'm glad Papina," Cederic commented. "And I'm glad Leke has been generous with his insights although his role here is not our counselor. I knew we all had some losses, so it made sense for us to talk about them. But I really didn't realize how much it would change my life also. I may not be the most talkative person here but having this place to come to has really helped me. Even though we get sad here, I am laughing more in life. It is as if the fact that I can talk about the pain of losing my mother has opened up a valve in me being able to talk about all the joy that she brought into my life. I am crying more but I am also laughing more, and I like it."

At this, a few people in the group laughed.

Ramatou commented:

"I agree. Even though our family is going through a hard time, I think we appreciate each other a little more. Adamou and I are trying to remember that our children are also grieving, and they are still here with us. We don't want to get so consumed by the child we've lost that we forget the ones who are here.

So, we have decided to do more things together as a family, spend more time talking and also going out as a family for fun. This has been good for us and the children. Adamou and I also decided that we want to keep the good memories of our son alive in the house. So, we often mention his name and try to tell stories about him. We think it is important that we start accepting the reality of life being different from how it was when he was here.

Our lives are not what they were when he was here and they will never be the same, but it doesn't mean that we cannot enjoy good things in life. Jesus still promises to give us abundant life and I believe it entails living full lives on earth.

Our suffering is suffering enough, we don't need to add to it by restricting ourselves from enjoying the good things even though there are painful things. So, we've been reminding the children of these things and helping them to do both grieving and playing. Amadou has found exercising very helpful and he's been taking the kids for 'daddy and the kids' workout times."

"Yes," Amadou interjected. "I noticed that working out helps me blow off steam. It's like a release for me, releasing pent up energy and stress. I feel really good after I work out. I was thinking about it and figured why don't I take the kids with me? Ramatou joins us sometimes too. I come up with a different plan of what we will do every week. Sometimes we go outdoors, sometimes it's indoors. We've been trying different things and I think it's been a good stress reliever. Don't you think, Ramatou?"

"Oh yes! The kids get excited about it and so do you, especially when you are doing your research for what to do. I think it is helping us to bond as a family and it's keeping us healthy, especially you and the kids. It's been great. It makes me realize another side of grief, which is connection.

It has allowed us to connect with each other and with God in ways that we could not have imagined before. It is true that God transforms us through our suffering. It hasn't been easy, but we are creating new things that we took for granted. For this, I am grateful."

Ramatou's sentiments resonated in the room as they exchanged a few more words before wrapping up the discussion with the plan to meet again in 2 weeks.

Resources for grief counseling and suicide loss survivors

The Mourners Bill of Rights https://healgrief.org/the-mourners-bill-of-rights/

Understanding Grief and Loss https://healgrief.org/understanding-grief/

National Suicide Prevention Lifeline https://988lifeline.org/

Jed Foundation. Emotional health and suicide prevention among teenagers and young adults. https://jedfoundation.org/

Alliance of Hope for Suicide Loss Survivors https://allianceofhope.org/find-support/find-a-support-group/

Suicide Support Group Locator https://afsp.org/find-a-support-group/

8

Male Depression And Workaholism

Today marks exactly two months since Jaward was rushed to the hospital by his wife, Tenneh, for what they initially thought was a heart attack but found out was a panic attack. It was frightening as well as relieving for Tenneh to be told that her husband was not dying; rather he was experiencing psychological distress.

Jaward, on the other hand, was upset. Even though he didn't want to have a heart attack, something about knowing he had a mental problem that had caused such a grave scare, repulsed him. He didn't like the thought of being associated with mental issues.

"Panic attacks are quite common, Mr. Kamara. Many patients come in mistaking panic attacks for heart attacks. Your heart is fine, but maybe you are going through some form of stress? Do you remember what happened before the onset?"

"No, doctor. I was sitting on the couch after a long day, then I felt a tightness in my chest and soon I was sweating, shaking, and felt like I couldn't breathe. It was as if I could hear my heart beating in my chest. That's when Tenneh walked in and saw me, but I couldn't respond to her."

"Do you remember experiencing something like this before?"

"No doctor, never in my life."

"Have things been stressful for you lately?"

"Isn't life always stressful?"

"Mr. Kamara, we will run some other tests just in case. In the meantime, may I have you speak with our behavioral health consultant? He can help talk you through other non-medical aspects that are going on in your life."

"Ok, no problem. Thank you, Dr. Jones."

Jaward remembers his brief exchange with Dr. Jones and then the behavioral health consultant, who recommended he come and talk to him in a week. Jaward didn't like hospitals. In fact, he had made it a goal of his not to be a frequent visitor to the hospital. At this point, he was fine with going in for his yearly check-up since Tenneh always insisted on it. That was the only reason he went.

Fortunately for him, he was a healthy 55-year-old man who appeared to have good genes. He wasn't aware of any family health conditions even though that may be partially due to the fact that like him, his parents never went to the doctor. Nevertheless, he rarely got sick and made it a point to engage in his daily run in the morning, he only drank alcohol socially, and slept for about 7 hours most nights. On paper, Jaward seemed healthy.

Hence, when Dr. Bah, the behavioral health consultant, told him to come back in a week, Jaward wasn't impressed. That would be twice in two weeks visiting a doctor. But then, he was happy to meet Dr. Bah, a fellow Sierra Leonean. What are the odds that he would meet a fellow country man in the hospital, a place he hates? Jaward thought it would give him another opportunity to see Dr. Bah, so why not.

"Hello Jaward," Dr. Bah greeted him with a smile on his face while stretching out his hand for a handshake. "It's good to see you again. How have you been?"

"I've been well, Dr. Bah. How are you?"

"Oh! I'm doing just fine, trying my best to live life." Dr. Bah had this warmness to him that made Jaward feel comfortable even though he was in a hospital still wondering why he was there. Jaward smiled at him, "That's good."

"Jaward, please call me Musa. I'm sure you are wondering why I called you in again."

"Actually, I was."

"I won't beat around the bush then. I think you will be a perfect candidate for our behavioral health program that I coordinate in this hospital. May I tell you about it?"

"Since I'm already here, why not? Go ahead."

"Great! I run a holistic men's health program in this hospital. During my 5 years working here, my colleagues and I have found that we see fewer men on a day-to-day basis, but when they do come to the hospital, the problems they present are at a more advanced level, meaning they weren't getting frequent check-ups or other preventative care. Or they come in due to scares, such as yours, that usually include a concerned family member bringing the man in just like your wife accompanied you last week. You see what I mean?"

Jaward nodded and Musa continued:

"Men have generally been found to be more self-reliant, to minimize their problems, and to manage their issues by themselves. They are also less likely to seek treatment for physical and mental health challenges. These problems are even more so among minority groups such as you and I. Men of color have higher rates of high blood pressure, heart disease, cardiovascular disease, prostate cancer, and other health conditions. They are also least likely to perceive their need for medical and mental health care, so they underutilize these services.[26]

So, we began asking ourselves, 'How can we get more men involved in the prevention, maintenance, and/or treatment of their health?' In case you didn't notice from our first meeting, my role in this hospital is focused on assisting with behavioral changes to improve your overall wellbeing. The medical staff such as Dr. Jones and behavioral professionals like myself work as a team to provide you with holistic healthcare. Is what I'm saying making sense so far?"

Jaward's thoughts were interrupted by Musa's question. It made perfect sense to him; he could relate to the men not using medical and mental services, after all he tried avoiding hospitals at all costs. "Yes, that makes sense although now it makes me wonder what your assessment was of me when we spoke last week."

Musa tilted his head back with a chuckle, "Jaward, you seem

to be a disciplined man in good physical shape. Dr. Jones didn't indicate any physical conditions of concern, which is a good thing probably helped by your current routines. The fact that you run almost every morning and you go to bed and wake up around the same time daily shows that you have some solid habits that have most likely been maintaining your wellbeing so far. However, from our chat last week, I got the sense that you may be struggling with depression and some anxiety. Do you remember the first thing you told me?"

"Vaguely."

"You said you can't remember the last time you were happy. You constantly feel worn out. Your work keeps you extremely busy most days leaving you no time to rest except at night. You said you are beginning to wonder if you can keep your job, which informed me that your work performance may no longer be as good as it used to be. Is that right?"

"I guess you can say so," Jaward felt a flush of embarrassment.

"I would like to add that your experience is not unusual. It is common for men to pour themselves into their work particularly during busy seasons as has been the case for you, right?"

"Yes, work has been extremely busy."

"Over-exerting oneself at work can further increase stress. In addition, even though you used to sleep throughout the night, lately, you've been waking up in the middle of the night and finding it hard to go back to sleep, which indicates sleep disturbance or stress. And you expressed that you have been drinking more alcohol lately. I gathered that you live with your wife and your 3 children, and you are the first child with 7 siblings all living back in Sierra Leone. You are the only one from your family of origin in the US."

"You have a good memory, Dr. Bah... Ehm... Musa."

"Well, thank you. I was just listening to you. I know how it is to have family back home that you are providing for. You said you are constantly moving such that even the times you have off are being taken up by your family in Sierra Leone seeking assistance from you in one way or another. It seems you have a lot of responsibilities that don't only involve your family here, but also providing for your extended family back home.

Being the first born, I can see why you believe that it is your duty to provide for your family. I can also see why you would be constantly tired or overwhelmed as you told me last week. You also indicated that you have lost interest in doing things you enjoyed doing including having sex with your wife.

Jaward, you may have been experiencing burnout for a long time, but I get the impression that you might now have symptoms of depression. You said you have been feeling this way for months now. In some ways, you having a panic attack was your body's cry for help, alerting you that something needs to change. You know our bodies are constantly finding ways to help us to survive and even thrive."

Jaward seemed slightly perplexed as he listened to Musa but began to draw some correlations between what Musa was saying and what his wife had been saying to him. When he met Musa for the first time last week, he surprised himself by being open about his life stressors. I guess he was tired of holding it all in for so long.

Musa had asked him many questions and was interested in

his answers. Jaward felt comfortable with him and found himself venting about how exhausting his life was. There weren't that many men in Jaward's life who were interested in listening to him, so it felt good talking to Musa.

Musa had suggested he slow down and reduce his workload if possible. Jaward had left the hospital feeling lighter after shedding off all the weight of worries from his mind. He reasoned that he could try to stop taking work so seriously and maybe that would ease some of his stress.

Now, looking at Musa, he felt a mixture of emotions. First, there was some discomfort from hearing the word "depression." What does this say about him? That he is too weak to manage his life? Second, there was the commitment to joining a program in a hospital. Who wants to come back to the hospital over and over again? Third, he liked Musa, he would get to see him again and talk to him, which might not be a bad idea. Fourth, would there be other men involved? How does this program work anyway?

"How does this program work?" was all he could muster up to ask.

"I'm glad you asked, Jaward. The program follows standard protocol for all the men involved with some personalized parts to it based on each man's needs. Currently, we have about 17 men and are hoping to get 24. We welcome men spreading the word to other men they know. We've seen that it can be beneficial to have your friends join you even though you will easily make friends throughout the program.

The standard protocol includes check-ups and screenings, health education on men's topics, male-bonding trips locally where we go hiking or do physical activities, group discussions, and one-on-one time with me to work on personal goals."

"For how long does this program last and how frequently do people meet?"

"We run a few programs each year, some simultaneously and at different times of the year. This one will be for 6 months. The activities are spread out through this period with a different activity weekly. So, you'll see me once a month one-on-one, male bonding activity once a month, group discussion once a month, health education once a month, and one medical check-up. We thought about making the program shorter, but we want the effects to stick so we've found it more advantageous having the program run for a longer period."

"Oh, I see. So, who pays for this Musa?"

"Another good question, nothing is really free in America, right? Well, we have worked out a partnership with a government funded institution whose main goal is to improve men's health engagement by the year 2040. This means that when you enroll in the program, your bills are waived, and they acquire all the expenses."

"Really?"

"Really! This is free for all men enrolled in the program. So, what do you say? Would you be interested in joining this program? We will begin in 3 weeks."

"Musa, I need to think about this."

"Of course. You don't need to respond right away but I will need an answer by next week."

"Okay."

"May I ask you why you hesitate though? What are your concerns?"

"Honestly?"

"Yes, please honesty is the best policy, right? Hahaha!"

"I'm concerned if I'll have the time to commit to this."

"Ok, what else are you concerned about?"

"Do I need it? What would it do for me?"

"Ok, what else, Jaward?"

"I like talking to you Musa, but I don't know if I care to talk to other men about my issues."

"Why is that?"

"Well, what's the point? Plus, I don't like coming to the hospital. And you are saying that I have depression. No one else is going to know about this, right?"

"Jaward, this seems to be the main problem, right? You feel a little embarrassed and maybe even concerned that you having depression makes you less of a man."

Jaward lowered his gaze with an expression that said "true" even though he didn't say anything.

"Not at all! It makes you human. Welcome to the experience of living in an imperfect world where there is physical and mental illness. If you broke your leg, would you go to the hospital and wear a cast if needed? If you had a heart disease, would you take medication and other treatment to improve your heart condition? So why is it different for your mental health? Why won't you do what you can to be mentally healthy?

Aside from that, think of depression again as your body's alarm telling you that there is something off that you need to pay attention to. Depression can be a symptom of other problems in your life, which I appreciate that you openly shared with me last week. You can thank your body for alerting you that the challenges you are facing are becoming too much for you to carry, so it will be helpful for you to share the load or find better ways to cope. This is where the men's program comes in.

We offer you people to share your burdens with and tools to help you deal with your stress. And you get all of this at no cost. It costs you nothing except your time each month for the next 6 months. But if you add up all the times we meet, it isn't that much especially because of how much more this program will bring into your life.

We have run this program for the past 3 years and I have yet to find one man who has left feeling worse than before they joined. Most of the reports I have received from previous attendees are improved relationships with their families, feeling less alone in managing their responsibilities, having more tools to cope with challenges, having a better understanding of their health, and some have gone on to form good friendships with other men in the program.

Regarding time commitment, the most you have to do is reserve 1 to 2 hours a week except for the day trips, which might take longer but you'll be glad for it. This is one of the favorite activities for the men. We have selected men whom we believe will benefit the most from the resources we provide, so you will find that you may be able to relate with the other men and they to you. Our goal is to bring men together with similar yet slightly different circumstances so that you can easily connect and learn from each other. So Jaward, you'll be in good company."

"Ok Musa, I still need some time to think about it and talk it over with my wife."

"Absolutely, smart man talking it over with your wife."

They both laughed.

"Here is my card. When you decide please give me a call and let me know and we can go from there. It's been a pleasure, Jaward," Musa said, extending his hand for a handshake.

"Thank you, Musa. Maybe I will see you around."

"I do hope so."

Today marks exactly two months since Jaward was rushed to the hospital by his wife, Tenneh. That makes one month since the men's program started. Jaward didn't expect to already feel so rejuvenated after one month. He was beginning to feel more pleasure again, and an increased sense of hope. He even thought, "the hospital is not that bad after all." And to think all this started because of a panic attack.

Chapter References

[26] American Psychological Association. (2018). APA guidelines for psychological practice with boys and men.

[26] Harper, J. (2021, July). Too many men ignore their depression, phobias, other mental health issues. Retrieved from https://www.washingtonpost.com/health/mental-health-men/2021/07/02/9a199734-d5e5-11eb-ae54-515e2f63d37d_story.html

9

Racism In Higher Education

Nanyamka finally made it to a Black Anthropology Graduate Student (BAGS) meeting. Honestly, she had been too busy to attend these meetings prior, but four things prompted her to tune in during this time. The first was personal, she was seeking validation from her own difficult year with the comprehensive fiasco that made her take a year off from her PhD.

The second was she heard that other Black students had had similar experiences and were thus collecting stories. The third was to see how this group was responding to the examination of conscience going on after the global outrage over George's Floyd's death. The fourth was that everything was virtual due to the COVID-19 pandemic, so she had the time and easy access.

Who knew that it would take such an egregious offense to

help her see that part of what had happened to her was attributed to racism? She thought it was just some power-hungry young man who was jealous of an accomplished junior colleague. But now sitting in various meetings held by her department, she realized that an important figure in the department, a professor, Dr. White, was considered by other minority faculty and students as racist.

She wasn't the first person of color he had discriminated against. He was now being openly called out by not only students but his colleagues as well. She wouldn't have thought that of him or her Dissertation Chair who was also being called out for discrimination. She found it odd that he opted to speak briefly with her on the phone, he was always dismissive, and he didn't give her valuable feedback. This was quite a contrast to her former thesis chair who was very willing to meet with her face to face and always provided helpful insights. Nanyamka sometimes felt like she was moving around in circles with her dissertation chair. Just her luck that the people who had power to help her advance in her PhD seemed to be in her way, fighting against her.

Well, now things were coming out in the open. Dr. White couldn't take the humiliation and had given his resignation. Can you imagine that the department chair refused the resignation, saying that he had apologized and learned his lesson? What about all the students along the years that he had hurt by being racist? How has he learned a lesson because he was being called out after several years of damage done? Giving him grace for repeated bad behavior without any repercussions for it, this would never happen if this man were Black, never!

The meeting was in progress, and it had come to her turn, "So Nanyamka, tell us what happened and feel free to give us some background on yourself. We like to know where people come from, it helps us understand their perspective," said the facilitator.

"Ok, my name is Nanyamka and I'm probably older than most people in the room. I am a proud wife, mother of 6 grown children who are all well-accomplished. And I am also a proud grandmother of 10. I moved to the US from Ghana about 7 years ago with my husband. My children were already here, they came a long time ago for college. I guess we wanted to experience life in America and be closer to our children and grandchildren.

My husband is semi-retired although he won't stop working. Back home in Ghana, I was a professor teaching History. It's rather unfortunate that America doesn't recognize foreign degrees especially those from Africa, I wouldn't have had to start from scratch here after being a full-time professor in Ghana for several years. Even the system is built to discriminate against certain countries, but I digress. There is no use crying over spilled milk. I had already decided to get another PhD in Anthropology but this time in the US. Even though starting a PhD at 65 years old is not easy, I was determined and even excited. The kids are all adults now, I can care for my grand babies and go to school."

The facilitator commented, "Welcome to BAGS. It's good to see more Africans here. We created this space for all Black students, but we realize that mostly African Americans come here, so we are glad to see you and more Africans join us."

Nanyamka continued, "Thank you my brother. Life is just so

busy and being used to a different system in Ghana, I don't know much about organizations on campus. You know we Africans who migrate we don't struggle much with race because we grew up in societies where Black people are majority. So, we don't think so much about how racism affects us personally. Or when we think about it, we shrug it off. We are not as racially conscious as say Black people who were born and raised in America. That's my opinion at least."

"Hm! I get what you mean," one of the board members said.

"Interesting, I hadn't thought of that," another person commented.

"So let me tell you what happened... I got an email 2 years ago saying I should come in person to talk about my PhD comprehensive exams. I didn't know what to expect but I walked into the professor's office, and he told me to sit down. He took out a folder from his desk. Then, he told me I plagiarized in my exam; so, he had no choice but to fail me.

I asked him how I had plagiarized, and he showed me marked sections saying I used exact words or just changed a few words. He had printed the papers I cited. I asked him if I could see the sections and he said I could look at them on my own time. I asked him if he had graded the paper and he said it didn't matter because I had failed. Since he was grading two of my exams, I asked whether my other exam had problems and he said yes but not many. I tried to inquire about when the check for plagiarism was done because I thought it was done before grading and he said yes, he had it before and then he did it again after he graded because the graders don't really check. So, I asked for scores, and he said it didn't matter because I had failed.

I was confused because that meant he had graded it, but it seemed he was withholding information and not wanting to engage with me about what exactly I had done and how I could make it better. I insisted before he told me my scores, which were passing scores. He told me my penalty for plagiarism was repeating both courses next spring, that is a year from the time. I asked him if I couldn't repeat it the next semester and he said no. He stated that he wanted to throw me out of the program, but he spoke to another faculty member, and she said that was too extreme because no one has received that penalty for the same offense.

He said nobody else knows about my alleged plagiarism because he is trying to prevent the stigma on me. So, he won't put it in my permanent record. He said some other things that at this point, I don't even remember because I was in shock. Throughout my 3 years in the program so far, I had never had an issue with plagiarism. And like I said, I was a professor in Ghana, I know what it means to plagiarize.

Again, I was shocked and was asking myself how I let this happen and why he was so dismissive as he spoke, telling me he wanted to throw me out as if he was doing me a favor by keeping me here. It's almost as if he wanted me to bow down and thank him for having mercy on me. He said I could appeal the decision by talking to the head of the department. So, I said thank you and left.

When I looked at the things he highlighted, I noticed that I may not have communicated the material in a concise manner because my goal was to give specific examples, but I don't believe it was plagiarism. I know what plagiarism is and I had not had that issue in the past. My plan was to appeal it, so I had a meeting with another professor and showed her my papers and asked for her opinion. She said some of the highlighted items had poor paraphrasing, but I didn't pass off the ideas as mine, all of them were cited. From her analysis, she didn't think I had plagiarized. Plus, there was evidence from the other papers I had written that I hadn't plagiarized in the past.

I was very angry because this was an attack on my integrity, my character and I didn't like that. Plus, I know that a good approach for professors to help students when they are in trouble academically is to give the student support or mentorship on how to address the issue. And this man had done quite the opposite."

"Why does this story sound very familiar?" The facilitator asked.

Khadija responded, "Because it is my story that I shared last week. It is literally the same experience I had with I'm guessing you are talking about Dr. White. He told me I plagiarized and when I pointed out that I didn't think I did, he said I don't understand what plagiarism is and that he thought about kicking me out but decided not to. I couldn't even fathom what he was saying especially because I had completed a Master's in Public Health in a different department in this same school and never had any problems. I also decided to take my work to be reviewed by my previous thesis chair to see if I had plagiarized. She told me she didn't think I did. She pointed to the fact that I had been successful in another program in this school."

"And the whole time I thought it was just me," Namyanka

said shaking her head. "That's too bad these things are happening repeatedly in this program."

Khadija spoke again, "Namyanka! Please continue your story. What did you do?"

"I tried to have a meeting with the head of the department, but he asked to speak on the phone. During the call, he wasn't quite interested in what I had to say and interrupted me when I was explaining. So, I thought this won't be helpful. I decided to write to the professor, Dr. White, which led to us having a meeting with four of the faculty.

It was the most disappointing discussion I have ever had. No one had any real empathy. The head of department took it as an opportunity to lecture me as if I was a teenager who had cheated on an English test. And then at the end of the meeting they asked me, 'Do you feel better?' How was I supposed to respond to that? 'No, I feel horrible,' is what I really wanted to say but I told them, 'Not really, but does it matter?' As if they cared how I felt. For them, they were glad they had done their job and put me in my place.

So, my conclusion was that I will sit quietly and lick my wounds, as my husband would say. I didn't feel like I had any support to go through an appeal, not from my chair or my advisor. I felt defeated and helpless, so I decided to take a break from school for the year."

The facilitator asked, "What about the other professor who had reviewed your paper? Could she intervene?"

"She is someone I worked for in a different department, so unfortunately she couldn't."

Khadija spoke again, "It is interesting because I can tell the difference between the health department and this one. I felt more at ease and supported there. Things have felt off here since I started my PhD."

The facilitator spoke, "That is one of the reasons why we created BAGS because many minority students have struggled in this department. You would think as anthropologists, we would be better at building healthy communities, but we're not. Not in here."

"The thing that made me even angrier afterward is that Dr. White wrote to the whole faculty and told them that I had failed my Comps since it was very uncommon for students to fail. I would have felt better if he gave them an explanation, but he didn't tell them anything about plagiarism.

It made me wonder if he wasn't sure about the plagiarism or if he was just trying to let them think I am not smart enough to make it through this program. All in all, it just seemed more obvious that he set out to hurt me. For someone to set out to hurt another to the maximum extent within his authority is scary. The expression, 'Green snake in green grass' was never more apparent.

For someone whom I have told people is nice, it beats me how I could not have been more perceptive. I thought I had a better judgment of human nature and situations than that. I have wondered where I really went wrong. It could not just be poor paraphrasing in an exam because others surely had the same issue. I have asked myself if I was so wrong in being so enthusiastic about getting a PhD in Anthropology. What else could he have done if I had already gone past my Comps stage when my unknown problem with him started? What hurt did I cause him?"

The facilitator spoke up, "There are subtle attacks that happen to minority graduate students that make them doubt themselves and leave them feeling what you expressed, Nanyamka. And many students don't feel supported at times like these, which contributes to delayed graduation periods for minority students and in some cases, dropouts."

"Nanyamka, as hard as it is when your intellect and your integrity are in question, we cannot take it personally. There is too much at stake. We need you to continue to fight to complete your degree," said a young woman in attendance.

"You know most of us have a story of difficulty going through graduate school. Sometimes, it is the mere fact that we are in graduate school, and it is hard. Sometimes, it is the fact that we are the first person in our families to make it this far in our education. Sometimes, it is our professors who can't seem to see past the color of our skin or our accents. They say we have to work twice as hard just to make it," said the facilitator.

Nanyamka spoke again, "I hear you. I hear you. The last meeting was very helpful because it helped me to see that there are multiple problems. One of them is that plagiarism policies are mostly punitive than corrective. They don't provide students with supportive resources. So how then can students get better?

The second thing that was striking is that it was the first time I thought of race as a potential factor in this complication with my Comps. I have always thought not to think about race, and I raised my 6 children to do the same. But that again goes to the fact that I didn't grow up here, so I haven't had to think about that in my day-to-day life. At least that's what I thought until recently, although my children used to tell me all the time that race is a big deal in America.

I found it enlightening when you said you were going to compile a list of those who have been victims of plagiarism accusations to see if there is any racial bias and disparity. Do you think this is what may have prompted Dr. White's resignation?"

"I don't know, but that's telling us something if he is tempted to resign when we announce looking at evidence."

"Well, that was the first time I thought of myself as a potential victim of racism that cost me an academic year of graduate school."

The facilitator expressed, "Thankfully you decided to come back. You are one of three people present today who have been accused of plagiarism. Another student was accused, and the situation was so poorly handled that she dropped out last year. Apart from plagiarism, Dr. White has received several complaints like having double standards for Black and White students. He would make comments such as calling the White students 'passionate and emotional' and the Black students 'aggressive and irrational.'

Then, there is the issue of funding. It is unclear who gets funding and why; there have been up to six Black graduate students who were promised funding then later told that there was a mix up. The saddest story is a Black woman who lost her funding because she was 8 months pregnant. She went through so much stress to try to keep her funding only to be told that there is no university law to accommodate her. Meanwhile a White student who was pregnant was accommodated and kept her funding. And to think that Dr. White is being rewarded for this by them refusing to let him resign. Such injustice!"

"Yes, many people have reported him to the department chair and the response has been that he was put in this position to learn and change. How convenient!" Nanyamka said.

"How so very convenient and outrageous if you think about it. It makes you wonder where we are and why this is still happening in 2020," Khadija said.

The facilitator then said, "And this is why we have organizations like BAGS and other Black student unions. We understand that educational success for Blacks and other minority students is not always straight-forward. Therefore, we hope to foster a community where we can support one another and bring our challenges to the forefront before they cause too much damage.

We hope that more people will continue to use this resource. We aim to present our concerns to higher authorities; we want to speak on your behalf when concerns arise, that is why we like to understand your stories. You can always reach out to us if you need support. We hope you know and feel that BAGS got your back. You are not alone in your experiences in this university. Thanks for sharing your story with us Nanyamka."

Contentment In Singleness

It was a celebration. Emekeng had just completed her Master's in Engineering and her parents were proud. In fact, every relative was proud, even the ones she hadn't seen for years were coming out of the woodwork to tell her how proud they were. Some offered unsolicited advice saying the next step was for her to get married.

She didn't understand why they all of a sudden felt they had a say in her status, or in her life for that matter. Why did they care anyway? It wasn't as if they were happily married themselves. And even if they were, they didn't know her. How many of them actually knew what was going on in her life other than that she was graduating? It seemed odd, this semblance of family that had no clue what was really going on...

"Eme," her thoughts were interrupted by an uncle whom she hadn't seen in 5 years.

"Yes uncle…"

"I haven't seen you in a long time. Congratulations again! You are making us proud."

"Thank you, uncle," Eme said politely as she smiled.

"How are the others? What is Mafua studying again?" he asked about her sister.

"She graduated over 7 years ago, she's working now."

"Oh! What about ehm… the other one…"

"Atabong? He's also working…"

"Oh really? Wow!" He looked perplexed and didn't know how to continue the conversation but felt the need to comment, "I didn't realize that you are all grown up and marriage material."

There it was again, marital status. I guess Africans just can't help themselves bringing it up, she thought. As if being married is what made her a person. She just finished pursuing a difficult yet enjoyable degree. Granted, her parents were relieved that it was one of the accepted degrees among African parents.

She was one of the few women in her class and one of two Black women. Aside from all that, she loved engineering and she believed she had a calling to use it to better the lives of others especially those on the African continent. She didn't know all the details of how, but she trusted God will make it clear in due time. As of now, she was excited to have graduated and about to begin her career. It took her some time to figure it out, but here she was. Unfortunately, her excitement was met with other people's concern for her marital status. Such a pity because many of them didn't understand.

They didn't know how content she finally felt to be single, no boyfriend, no husband, no children, just her and PAPA. Such a wonderful place of freedom to love and serve whoever she wanted. While others were scurrying around trying to project their own insecurities on her, she was at peace loving being a single 33-year-old woman.

Emekeng didn't know if she wanted to get married anymore and she didn't care. She knew that wherever she ended up, single, married, or married with children, her life was going to be good because PAPA could fulfill all her needs. She didn't need anything else or anyone else to be more complete. She was complete in Jesus. Her identity was in him alone. She didn't even need to give birth to have children because she could have as many spiritual children as she wanted.

Emekeng had come to understand that God would not withhold anything from her because of her status. He could give her companionship with friends who loved and cared for her as she did them. She understood how it felt to be loved romantically by her ex-boyfriend and somehow that fulfilled her need for romance. PAPA took her out of that relationship just at the right time and He redirected her focus to Him, the lover of her soul.

She didn't even need to have sex because PAPA had fulfilled those desires as well and replaced any sensual urges with Himself. It was really a mystery, but such are the promises of her PAPA. As a celibate single in Christ, she had everything she needed, and she felt good about fulfilling her purpose. Emekeng knew that many people, even followers of the same Jesus, would have a problem with her telling them these things. But she was convinced and only PAPA could tell her differently.

Although she hadn't always thought this way, it is true what Romans 12:2 says, "Do not conform to the pattern of this world but be transformed by the renewing of your mind. Then you will be able to test and approve what God's will is—his good, pleasing and perfect will.[27]" Life had given her many opportunities to test and approve God's will. Her life had been transformed and she no longer fell for the thinking of the world. She believed God's Word.

13 years prior to graduation

Emekeng remembers that God had been pursuing her long before she accepted his proposal. The first time she audibly heard His voice was when she was in college. She had decided to stop messing around with guys and prayed for God's help with loneliness. The whisper she heard told her to sleep in the middle of her queen-size bed rather than at the side, as if she were waiting for someone to fill it. This simple adjustment to her sleeping position made a shift, relieving some of those lonely feelings she experienced. The journey of reclaiming her life in God had begun.

10 years prior to graduation

Papa was already a common name to her because that's how she called her father. She also heard many of her relatives pray saying, "Papa God." However, her relationship with God didn't feel personal until she truly came to understand what Jesus did for her. That even if she were the only one on the earth, he would have gone through all that he went through just for her. Such sacrificial love!

Emekeng was moved and chose to repent, get baptized, and live a life for him. She decided to give up her lustful ways and abandon herself to being a celibate single living for Him. Emekeng adopted the name PAPA for how she would refer to God[28] and thought it was fitting that the name was how she would call her father, but it was all in capital letters to signify His grandeur.

9 years prior to graduation

She remembers lying on her bed and she heard a whisper, "I'm proud of you baby." It seemed strange this time, almost louder. PAPA was telling her that he was proud of her for standing up for her convictions. She didn't want people getting drunk in her apartment, so when some friends started having too many drinks at her place, she said the party was over and sent them home.

A friend of hers had said, "Oh come on Eme, it's your party, don't be a downer." She didn't care. What would she tell PAPA afterward? That she allowed people to over-indulge and sin under her own roof when she could help it? She wasn't having it. It was time for them to go home. Later that night as she lay in her bed, that's when she heard His voice. She smiled. She even got a little giddy. PAPA was talking to her, and He called her "baby." She pictured herself as a little girl looking up at the one she was growing to love.

6 years prior to graduation

The desire to get married was getting stronger. Emekeng had now been in 5 bridal parties of friends and relatives. As happy as she was to see them get married, there was always some dreaminess of when it would be her turn.

But it was complicated for her. Thinking of marriage as an African immigrant brought up conflicting feelings of living in two worlds, Africa and America. She wanted to return to some place in Africa even if it wasn't her home country, but she was getting more comfortable in the U.S. It had been almost 8 years since she came to the U.S. for college, and she wasn't sure how she would adjust to a life back home. Nevertheless, it was still home, and she loved it. And what if she finds someone who wants to spend the rest of his life in America? Would that be a deal breaker? Can she find a partner who understands both worlds and wants to live in Africa someday? This struggle made looking for a partner challenging.

Some of her African friends had gone back to their countries and gotten married, others had found a spouse from home and returned to the U.S. She saw relatives find a fellow African living in the U.S. and get married. Sometimes, it happened so quickly that she wondered why they were rushing. Still others found love regardless of culture.

Emekeng always thought it was easier for her White friends in the U.S. because they didn't have to navigate between cultures, they had more options. She found that immigrants had more of a challenge while trying to figure out where to reside. To add to that, it was important for her to find a spouse who took his faith in Jesus seriously. She wasn't willing to settle just because she met some man with whom she had something in common. She wanted a real partnership. And most of all she wanted a relationship that would honor PAPA.

Emekeng stumbled upon the book on praying for your future husbands[29]. She read it twice. The first time on her own and the second time with a group of friends. They read and prayed. She wrote her list. Yes, the famous list that we like to write about what we want in a partner. She still has that list, but when she looks back, she realizes that PAPA used every opportunity to draw her closer to Him. That season was about connecting with PAPA and His heart. She knows now that PAPA knows what she needs.

3 years prior to graduation

She met him, a man from her hometown. They had chemistry, they had similar interests, they had shared vision for the future, and it was an instant connection. It felt like she had known him for a long time. He had many qualities she admired. He was generous, kind, gentle, passionate about helping the poor, hard-working, and very in-tune with the people around him.

Emekeng initially turned him down because he wasn't too sure about living for Jesus. But he was open. After multiple Bible studies, discussions, prayers, and fasting, she thought there could be something here. But the relationship didn't work. Emekeng was back to being single again. However, God had done something good. He allowed her to experience what it felt like to be genuinely pursued and loved by a man. Even if that was all he wanted her to get from this experience, it was worth it.

He gave her the opportunity to test her faith and approve the Lord's will. She learned that some relationships were not meant to last but only to teach us lessons we would need for the future. It is not always a bad thing when a relationship ends, and it doesn't always mean the relationship should not have happened in the first place. As difficult as it was to go through, Emekeng didn't feel heart-broken, she felt loved by someone greater. God used this relationship to show Emekeng what a partnership could look like and somehow that satisfied some of her need to be married.

The night of graduation

As Emekeng lay in her bed after the festivities and the reminders of her singleness, she felt it necessary to journal as she usually does:

Dear PAPA,

I am grateful for everything you have done. Thank you for my family and friends who love me and came today. Thanks for allowing me to graduate. I'm looking forward to our life together, you and I PAPA. Right now though, I want to vent.

The thing I hate the most about these parties is the reminder of my status. Most societies put pressure on single people to get married, but for our people, that pressure is just too much. Why don't all these people go and look at their own marriages instead of pressuring us to get married?

Is it just a matter of them being able to say, "I'm married?" Nah which kind palava be this one[30]? See me see trouble[31]! I mean I can understand that the whole premise of collectivism is prioritizing groups, so how can I do that as an unmarried person? And what happens to the family name if it ends with me? But You changed all that when Jesus came.

It doesn't matter anymore, right? Isn't that the whole reason why

You came? Why are Christian parents so afraid that their children won't get married? What's the fear? It's not about us or our seed anymore. It's about Jesus and his seed. When the people told Jesus that his mother, (a whole Mami Mary) and his siblings were outside, didn't he say to the crowd that whoever does Your will is his brother, sister and mother? Why would he choose Your followers over his own blood family if he wasn't trying to prove a point? His point is we have new families in You through the church. Thank You for that by the way. You were thinking of all of us.

Yet, we are still so fearful of not getting married, of not having blood children. In the beginning, You wanted us to multiply, to fill the earth in number, but now You want us to multiply and fill the earth with the gospel. Why are we so afraid of being single? Am I the only one reading 1 Corinthians 7 or the New Testament? Wasn't Jesus single? Wasn't Paul single? Didn't Paul prefer singleness? I'm grateful that You don't care if we are married or single, You want all of us to fulfill our purpose using both of these gifts, the gift of singleness and the gift of marriage.

You don't rate singleness or marriage as lower than the other. In Christ, we are all one. To You, being single or being married with or without children is a good thing. No one is above the other, we are all on equal status before You. Being married is a gift, it's not an accomplishment. Marriage is a gift like singleness is a gift. I don't walk around telling married people to reject their gift, why do they walk around telling me to reject mine? They try so hard to get us married instead of helping us to be holy. Isn't that the goal? To be more like Jesus?

People like projecting me into a future that they don't understand, trying to rush Your process when they don't know where I've been. And then they want me to claim their so-called blessings by saying "amen" when they don't know what God has already been doing in my heart and life.

It is as if the goal for them is the physical manifestation of wealth, marriage, and children, but I believe the goal is for each one of us to look more like Jesus in whatever situation. What will help me look more like Jesus is different from what will help someone else. It could be marriage for me, it could be singleness for someone else. We need to stop projecting our desires unto others and ask them more questions to understand what God is doing in their lives. We are so quick to give advice without understanding.

And why do people make it such a taboo when others don't have children? I think some people just want to have children to be able to say that they have children. They don't actually care to parent, when others who have never had their own biological children are great parents to many.

I've seen several childless people care for many children. You know, like Aunty Yaya who started the children's choir and Aunty Ngwa who always has children in her home that she feeds and even pays for their education. How different is that from being a parent? Don't each of those kids carry with them pieces of these aunties with them?

Why do we worry so much about things that You have provided solutions for? Jesus lives on and on even though he had no physical children. Paul lives on and on even though he had no physical children. When I read the New Testament, the person who seemed to have the most (spiritual) children than everyone else was the unmarried childless Paul.

I can see that Paul, just like these two aunties had a lot more to give to others. That's one of the reasons You value each of us however we are, single, married, or married without children. Because each *situation makes different things possible. No matter where we are, we can fulfill various needs for the communities in which we live. We can have impact in the world, and we can still help people to know You.*

PAPA, it annoys me sometimes that we miss the point. But I'll stop venting. I think I've gotten all my anger out. PAPA, I'm glad that You are a Father that welcomes all my thoughts no matter how crazy they sound.

Do you remember when Anyi told me that whomever she marries will be a step down from having a perfect lover? That our loyalties are divided as a married person because we are concerned for the welfare of our spouses, which can distract from our loyalties to You[32]? I don't want that.

I love our life together and I do like marriage too, I just don't think it is greater than singleness. And I know You don't either. At the same time, I don't want to be a marriage-basher and a singleness-lover; I want to have a balanced view of both, seeing that both of them are equally good. I also don't want people telling me how to feel about where I am because right now, I like where I am, and it's taken me a long time to get here.

I like what Tony Evans said in his book, Living Single[33], "God knows where you live." He's right, You know where I live and You know what I need. Paul preferred being single because he could be fully devoted to You. I've seen people's devotion be divided because they constantly worry about meeting a partner. I don't want that.

I want to be found while I am fully devoted to You. I want to be about my Father's business and if I find someone, great. If I don't find someone, great too. I get to enjoy You all the more. I said I was going to stop venting, but here I am, sorry PAPA. I think I got it all out for now.

I thank You that I was created for You. That you looked at the whole wide world and decided that I will be here in this day and age. You knew me even before my mother did and You love me no matter what.

I thank You that I am dark, lovely and curvaceous. I love the way You made me. And can I just say I love my hair. I love how curly it is and that I can do so much with it. I love the reminders You give me of how wonderful and beautiful I am and that I belong to You.

I love my Africanness, all of it, even the things that others have despised. I know that You created me this way and I am so grateful. I am thankful to be a passenger in Your life. You own all of it and I won't be here 100 years from now. I'm grateful for that. I pray that while I am here, You will use me and continue to help me to focus on You. I love You, PAPA!

Your love, Eme

Chapter Notes

27 Romans 12:2 NIV

28 Also inspired by The Shack: Where Tragedy Confronts Eternity by William P. Young.

29 Tricia Goyer and Robin Jones Gunn. 2011. Praying for Your Future Husband: Preparing Your Heart for His. Published by Multnomah

30 In Cameroonian pidgin English meaning, "what kind of trouble is this?"

31 An expression in Cameroonian pidgin English alluding to something in the likes of "why do I have to be involved in this trouble?"

32 Paul described this in 1 Corinthians 7:32-24

33 Evans, Tony (2013). Living Single. Published by Moody Publishers.

Notes

1. ˆ In Cameroon and other parts of Africa, people who have severe mental illnesses are referred to as "mad man" or "man woman." "Mad" is equivalent to "crazy."
2. ˆ Speaking in Pidgin English meaning "Please, leave me."
3. ˆ Boni is short for Boniface
4. ˆ Agi is short for Agnes
5. ˆ Is an endearing phrase in French Africa that translates to "sweetheart" or "darling"
6. ˆ This is equivalent to 1st grade in elementary school
7. ˆ First level of examinations originating from British system and common in English speaking parts of Africa. This exam is the 1st of 2 to determine preparedness for university.
8. ˆ All girls Catholic boarding school in Bamenda, Cameroon
9. ˆ All boys Catholic boarding school in Bamenda, Cameroon
10. ˆ The second exam to determine preparedness for university
11. ˆ An expression for mother
12. ˆ An expression of empathy common throughout Cameroon
13. ˆ A popular Cameroonian dish of corn millet, vegetables, and chicken stew
14. ˆ Fornek, K. (2018, June). Murder-suicide in Darien connected to marital problems, police say. *Chicago*

Trubune. Retrieved from https://www.chicagotribune.com/suburbs/burr-ridge/ct-dbr-darien-murder-suicide-tl-0628-story.html

15. ˆ Mota, C. (2018, May). Days before murder-suicide, man threatened to send wife 'back to Africa in a coffin.' *The Jersey Journal.* Retrieved from https://www.nj.com/hudson/2018/05/days_before_murder_man_threatened_to_send_wife_bac.html

16. ˆ Sina, K. N. (2020, June). US Homicide : Chris /Annie Takam die in crime of passion. *CRTV.* Retrieved from https://www.crtv.cm/2020/06/us-homicide-chris-annie-takam-die-in-crime-of-passion/

17. ˆ Rice, K. (2020, September). Pastor who shot, killed wife threatened to kill her during argument the day before, Orlando police say. *Orlando Sentinel.* Retrieved from https://www.orlandosentinel.com/news/breaking-news/os-ne-new-details-killing-orlando-pastor-shot-wife-20200912-aqa4cqkoorf7vejly53k7nqxt4-story.html

18. ˆ Nwoye, I. C. (2017, July). The hotline trying to stop men murdering their wives. *Aljazeera.* Retrieved from https://www.aljazeera.com/features/2017/7/21/the-hotline-trying-to-stop-men-murdering-their-wives

19. ˆ A slang used in some African countries to describe someone (usually a fellow African) who has traveled abroad.

20. ˆ *John 3:8*

21. ˆ In Cameroonian pidgin English meaning, "I'm fine, grandmom. How are you?"

22. ˆ In Cameroonian pidgin English meaning, "I'm fine as well. How is school going?"

23. ˆ In Cameroonian pidgin English meaning, "School is going well. I will be graduating soon."

24. ˆ In Cameroonian pidgin English meaning, "Be well."

25. ˆ Liberman, Z., Woodward, A. L., Keysar, B., & Kinzler, K. D. (2017). Exposure to multiple languages enhances communication skills in infancy. Developmental science, 20(1), e12420.

26. ˆ American Psychological Association. (2018). APA guidelines for psychological practice with boys and men. Harper, J. (2021, July). Too many men ignore their depression, phobias, other mental health issues. Retrieved from https://www.washingtonpost.com/health/mental-health-men/2021/07/02/9a199734-d5e5-11eb-ae54-515e2f63d37d_story.html

27. ˆ Romans 12:2 NIV

28. ˆ Also inspired by The Shack: Where Tragedy Confronts Eternity by William P. Young.

29. ˆ Tricia Goyer and Robin Jones Gunn. 2011. Praying for Your Future Husband: Preparing Your Heart for His. Published by Multnomah

30. ˆ In Cameroonian pidgin English meaning, "what kind of trouble is this?"

31. ˆ An expression in Cameroonian pidgin English alluding to something in the likes of "why do I have to be involved in this trouble?"

32. ˆ Paul described this in 1 Corinthians 7:32-24

33. ˆ Evans, Tony (2013). Living Single. Published by Moody Publishers.

Acknowledgments

Dear PAPA,

Thank you! I'm grateful for every part of the journey we've been on to get here. Thanks for your amazing grace, love, and wisdom. Thanks for your creativity and for choosing me to partner with you to write this book. I feel so honored and amazed at how it all came together. You are amazing in how you help us realize and affirm our gifts. I thank you for all the people who helped me accept and use mine, all the people you used to get this book here, and all the people you will use to get the book to those whom you want.

I am grateful to my sister, Fuajia Amin and the creativity you gave her to design the book cover. Her ideas and designs have been instrumental throughout my journey with African Mind Healer. I continue to look forward to seeing what you are doing with her work in Salted Branding. I am grateful to my parents and siblings for always being supportive of my work. They have made it easy for me to explore, write, and create. I'm forever grateful to be a part of this family.

I am grateful for Oluwatosin Solarin's assistance these past years to believe in and share my work and ideas through various platforms.

Thank you Lord for my relatives, friends, and my church family. I'm grateful for the ways that they strengthen and encourage me in my faith and my life; for we cannot live this life alone and I'm glad you blessed me with all the people you've put around me.

I am especially grateful to you for my best friend, Deriise Dowell whose eye for editing and copywriting brought this book to another level. I am grateful to you for Manka'a Fontem whose proofreading skills cleaned up this book. I am so glad that they were the first two people to read the book and most of all that they got it! I'm grateful for their feedback.

I will be remiss if I don't thank you for my dissertation committee, Dr. Leihua Edstrom, Dr. Becky Sherman, and Dr. Rowlanda Cawthon whose encouragement to me to write a book from my research, was affirmation I needed.

Finally, I am grateful to my research participants who were vulnerable to share their lives with me. And I thank you for my clients and all the Africans who inspired the thoughts and stories in this book. It would not have been possible without them.

I look forward to working on more books with you.

Until then, your love!

~ Ajab

References And Further Readings

American Psychological Association. (2018). APA guidelines for psychological practice with boys and men.

Amin, A. (2018). *A Qualitative Study on Treatment Approaches and Culturally Sensitive Mental Care for African Immigrants in the U.S.* (Doctoral dissertation, Northwest University).

Evans, Toni. (2013). Living Single. Moody Publishers.

Fornek, K. (2018, June). Murder-suicide in Darien connected to marital problems, police say. *Chicago Trubune*. Retrieved from https://www.chicagotribune.com/suburbs/burr-ridge/ct-dbr-darien-murder-suicide-tl-0628-story.html

Goyer, T. & Gunn, R.J. (2011). Praying for Your Future Husband: Preparing Your Heart for His. Published by Multnomah.

Harper, J. (2021, July). Too many men ignore their depression, phobias, other mental health issues. Retrieved from https://www.washingtonpost.com/health/mental-health-men/2021/07/02/9a199734-d5e5-11eb-ae54-515e2f63d37d_story.html

Liberman, Z., Woodward, A. L., Keysar, B., & Kinzler, K. D. (2017). Exposure to multiple languages enhances communication skills in infancy. Developmental science, 20(1), e12420.

Mota, C. (2018, May). Days before murder-suicide, man threatened to send wife 'back to Africa in a coffin.' *The Jersey Journal*. Retrieved from https://www.nj.com/hudson/2018/05/days_before_murder_man_threatened_to_send_wife_bac.html

Nwoye, I. C. (2017, July). The hotline trying to stop men murdering their wives. *Aljazeera.* Retrieved from https://www.aljazeera.com/features/2017/7/21/the-hotline-trying-to-stop-men-murdering-their-wives

Rice, K. (2020, September). Pastor who shot, killed wife threatened to kill her during argument the day before, Orlando police say. *Orlando Sentinel.* Retrieved from https://www.orlandosentinel.com/news/breaking-news/os-ne-new-details-killing-orlando-pastor-shot-wife-20200912-aqa4cqkoorf7vejly53k7nqxt4-story.html

Sina, K. N. (2020, June). US Homicide : Chris /Annie Takam die in crime of passion. *CRTV.* Retrieved from https://www.crtv.cm/2020/06/us-homicide-chris-annie-takam-die-in-crime-of-passion/

Young, William P. (2007). The Shack: Where Tragedy Confronts Eternity. Windblown Media; First Edition.

Additional Resources

Resources on Sexual Assault

National Sexual Assault Hotline. RAINN. https://www.rainn.org/

National Sexual Violence Resource Center (NSVRC).
    https://www.nsvrc.org/survivors

Joyful Heart Foundation http://www.joyfulheartfoundation.org/

NotAlone https://obamawhitehouse.archives.gov/1is2many/notalone

VictimConnect Resource Center https://victimconnect.org/

Sexual Assault Kit Initiative (SAKI) https://www.sakitta.org/survivors/

Resources for Grief Counseling

Pathways Center for Grief and Loss https://www.hospiceandcommunity-care.org/grief-and-loss/grief-links/

The Mourners Bill of Rights https://healgrief.org/the-mourners-bill-of-rights/

Understanding Grief and Loss https://healgrief.org/understanding-grief/

Resources for Suicide Loss Survivors

National Suicide Prevention Lifeline https://988lifeline.org/

Jed Foundation. Emotional health and suicide prevention among teenagers
    and young adults. https://jedfoundation.org/

Alliance of Hope for Suicide Loss Survivors https://allianceofhope.org/
    find-support/find-a-support-group/

Suicide Support Group Locator https://afsp.org/find-a-support-group/

Ajabeyang Amin, PsyD, MPH is a lover of God and a Cameroonian American Psychologist. On her journey to obtaining her master's in public health, God redirected her path to counseling psychology where she discovered the joys and pains of walking alongside people. She founded African Mind Healer LLC where she writes and practices psychotherapy and Christian counseling. She was a recipient of the Brainz 500 Global Award in 2021 and was an Executive Contributor for Brainz Magazine from 2021-2022. Although born in Pennsylvania, she grew up in Cameroon and returned to the U.S. when she was 18 years old. Her personal and professional background contribute to her love for the intersection of faith, culture, and mental health, and their effects on our wellbeing. The stories in this book are inspired by her dissertation research on African immigrants in the U.S., connections with family and friends, and her own personal experiences.